Japanese Garden and Floral Art

HEARTHSIDE PRESS INC. • Publishers • New York

Mrs. Paul Kincaid

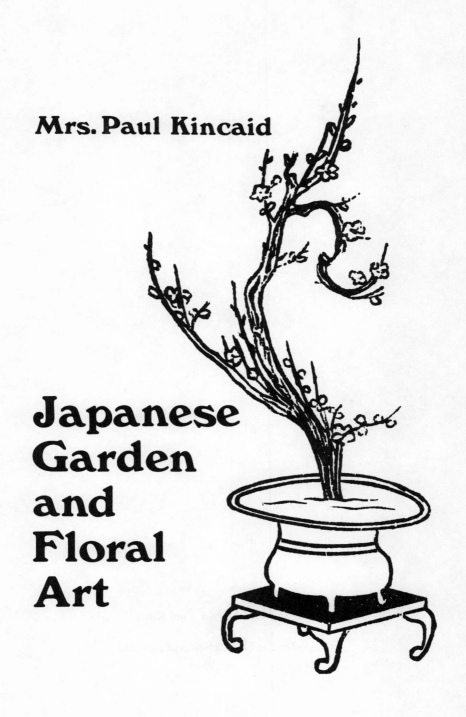

Japanese
Garden
and
Floral
Art

To my children
Paul Kincaid, junior
and Kay Kincaid Moss

ACKNOWLEDGMENTS

Without the assistance of my Japanese friends I would never have attempted a book such as this. I am especially indebted to the following:

Mr. Choca Adachi, Headmaster of Adachi-ryu; Mr. Katsuyuki Fugisawa; Mrs. Hatsue Harada; Mrs. Masumi Hayama; Mr. Mitsuo Horiguchi; Mr. Sen-ei Ikenobo, Headmaster of Ikenobo school of flower arrangement; Mr. Yasuo Inoue of Kokusai Bunka Shinkokai; Mr. Shun Kimiwada; Mrs. Keiji Nakamura; Mrs. Kazuko Ogura; Mr. S. Ozawa and Mr. Jintaro Takano.

Americans who have given me help and inspiration are Dr. George Avery of the Brooklyn Botanic Garden; Mrs. Alberta Queen, who typed the manuscript and voluminous correspondence; Mrs. Nedda C. Anders, Editor of Hearthside Press, Inc., who is the nicest possible person with whom to work; and my husband, Paul, who shares my hobbies and allows me to share his. He not only accepts my idiosyncracies but encourages them.

CONTENTS

AN INTRODUCTION TO
JAPANESE AESTHETICS

I

In all their arts the Japanese have been satisfied with nothing short of perfection. Perhaps that is why each branch of Japanese art merits universal interest. Their understanding of great lasting beauty surpasses that of any other culture. The cultural ways of Japan are restrained, nonemphatic, suggestive, understated and tranquil. Their centuries-old uninterrupted pursuit of beauty has meaning for our own lives regardless of the future course of history. Studying things Japanese will help exercise new powers of awareness and open your eyes to things you have missed.

In my studies of the Japanese floral arts I have been especially fortunate in having Japanese friends whose refined taste enabled me to acquire to some degree their cultural approach and the aesthetic appreciation necessary to an understanding of the subtle beauty of their art with flowers and plants. Because this book is broad in scope the treatment is necessarily compact. I have provided such historical and aesthetic aspects as are necessary for an appreciation of the subjects covered.

Although Japan received the initial knowledge and inspiration in her arts from China, through the centuries she has added a rich voice of her own which expresses native traditions and the aesthetic ideals of her people. The cultural history of Japan until the nineteenth century is in a sense the history of the spread of Chinese civilization to the Japanese islands and the reaction of the Japanese to it. The process whereby the culture of a great continental nation was adopted into a small insular kingdom was of necessity not simply a matter of copying. What was suitable and pleasing to the Chinese was usually unnatural and often totally alien to the islands, therefore the elements were reinterpreted, revised and at times rejected. The result was the creation of a Japanese culture which, while rooted in Chinese civilization, is an entity in itself.

The Japanese possess the innate artistic sense to assimilate and adapt, absorb and nationalize that which they borrow.

From the sixth century until the ninth there was a period of intensive learning from China followed by centuries of assimilation and refinement of this knowledge. In the seventeenth century Japan closed up like an oyster until it was pried open two hundred years later. This time the influence was from the West and came in two explosive blasts. The first was triggered by Commodore Matthew Perry's fleet forcing its way into Tokyo Bay in July, 1853. Within one generation Japan changed from a feudal society to one of the leading industrial and military powers in the world. The second explosion was touched off by the proclamation of General Douglas MacArthur's "Initial Post-Surrender Policy for Japan" in August, 1945.

The years of awakening of Japan and development of the country along Western lines have much in common with the years following the introduction of Chinese civilization. The same intensity and zeal for knowledge has characterized the present period. If at times the emulation seems excessive it comes not so much from a desire to imitate as from an overeagerness to learn. In time the Japanese people will succeed in blending the East and West. It will take time and no one can tell what the New Japan will turn out to be. At present the hectic drive is to out-Americanize America.

Unfortunately, few visitors to Japan get beyond the Westernized facade of Tokyo and a few tourist attractions at Kyoto. Those who do are bewitched by the wonder and beauty of what remains of the old Japan and to witness its eventual destruction would be a grief to anyone who has felt its charm. The countless restrictions that once ruled this fairy-world and shaped the soul and heart of it led to the simplicity of old customs: amiable manners, dainty habits, delicate tact displayed in giving pleasure, the gift of presenting outwardly only the best and brightest traits of character under any circumstances. Despite our incapacity to enter the soul-life of this ancient land we are nonetheless charmed unspeakably by the fine natures of these people which have been forged by ancient Shintoism, Buddhism and Confucianism that exacted all that is noble, not less than all that is terrible, in duty, gratitude and self-denial. Old Japan came nearer to the achievement of the highest moral ideal than our very evolved societies can hope to do for centuries.

One is utterly charmed by the delicacy and differentness of Japan but with all the intriguing differentness there is no place where an aware, alive traveler can reap richer rewards in ideas and things with which to improve the beauty and quality of his way of life at home. Here is a sophisticated and elegant culture that has been developing for two thousand years. When our Western European ancestors were still nomadic tribes the Japanese had attained a high civilization and were communicating in poetry!

JAPANESE SENSE OF BEAUTY

The Japanese aesthetic sensibility rises to such a high level of refinement that their arts are replete with beauties often too subtle for casual Occidental perception. It is said that true beauty can be discovered only by completing the incomplete. One of the principal characteristics of Japanese art is that it leaves much unsaid. A remote illusion is often enough to satisfy a cultured Japanese. This quality of aesthetic appreciation owes much to Zen Buddhism in the cultural pursuits of tea ceremony, the art of garden design and flower arrangement. Zen philosophy teaches that the value of suggestion is of utmost importance in these and all the other arts because in leaving something incomplete the beholder is privileged to finish the scene according to his own imagination. Therefore, a great masterpiece holds the viewer's attention and he feels he is a part of it. The practice of Zen is realized in the gentle teasing charm of

1. Shibui, *a word expressive of the highest level of beauty, can be attained only by restraint and understatement. This quiet garden scene exemplifies it.*

incompleteness. Zen accepts the mundane world as it is and tries to find beauty in our world of worry and woe, his world of earthquake and typhoon. We cannot overemphasize the importance of Zen and the tea ceremony which it engendered and the role they have played in creating a uniquely Japanese sense of beauty. *Kirei,* the standard term for beautiful in Japan, means clean and pure.

A Japanese garden or flower arrangement gets a greater color effect with few bright blossoms and leaves of a variety of sizes, textures and shades of green than a Westerner is able to accomplish with wide abundance of colored flowers arranged in large masses. The Japanese feel that bright colors tire the eye but the subtlety of greens rests it.

The arts of gardening and flower arrangement can be characterized by the noun *shibusa* or the adjective *shibui.*

Shibui

If *shibui* is not a part of your vocabulary do include it. You will find a new dimension in the world of beauty and you will see things that you missed before. You will develop a new and delicate perception and learn to see and grasp the total picture rather than mere fragments. *Shibui* is the deepest and purest beauty word in the world. There is no single word in the English language which adequately defines it but it is easily understood if you pursue its meaning. In pursuing and understanding it you will gain a new set of values for thinking about all kinds of beauty and your judgement will be sharpened and deepened.

Shibui is a discriminating artistic taste which has been described as neither sweet nor sour but gently astringent, which avoids and suggests them both. If you take the essence of the following words and phrases you will have an idea of the meaning of *shibui:* quiet taste and elegance, refined simplicity, culture, a great consideration for others, serenity, modesty, formality, restraint and nobility.

Shibui can apply to objects, manners of conduct, personal dress, gardens, flower arrangement, food—actually to all phases of living. Anything *shibui* is never obtrusive or ostentatious but presents a profound unassuming, quiet feeling.

An important part of *shibui* is incompleteness and imperfection. Nothing that is flawless, absolutely complete, and perfect can be *shibui.* We must remember that man and life have limitations, nothing is perfect and we can't have everything we may want just as we would like it to be. In a flower arrangement a leaf is often deliberately torn to serve as a reminder of the imperfection of life.

The idea of worship and reverence for life, for nature and the natural order of things is behind the word *shibui.* There is a balance between discipline and freedom that gives "things Japanese" their serenity, the quality of *shibui.*

Wabi and Sabi

Like *shibui, wabi* and *sabi* have depths of meaning that literal translations do
not convey. We cannot understand their meanings unless we reach beyond literal
translations and grasp the spirit of the words. The words *wabi* and *sabi* came into
use from the teachings of Sen-no Rikyu and the philosophic frame of mind that
became the main purpose of the tea ceremony. This frame of mind consists of a
mental attitude in which people in mutual humility esteem each other as equals,
and an atmosphere in which people, using various manners and movements,
embody this attitude in tastes for the tea room, the tea garden, the flower arrangement and the tea utensils. In short this attitude is expressed in subdued tastes
for quiet elegance, *wabi* and *sabi.*

Wabi, a very abstract concept, describes the atmosphere of quietness, tranquility, astringency, humbleness (humble by choice not by necessity), aloneness,
and harmonious yet unbalanced beauty.

2. *(Left) A lonely camellia tree in a sea of raked gravel illustrates the* wabi
concept of beauty with its hint of sadness.

3. *(Right) An ancient purification stone designed in the manner of a Chinese
coin and a moss-covered stone lantern display the* sabi *concept of beauty
based on the much desired patina of age.*

Sabi means unobtrusive and patinated by use and age. The concept of *sabi* is not strange to us since we too prize the patina and bloom of time we find on antiques.

The Japanese love the unpainted grain of wood, surfaces that have weathered to a soft grey, rocks that are covered with moss and lichens, the old colors of roof tiles, mud plaster, rough pottery, rustic fences, and *tatami* mats. Wooden fence posts and tree supports are frequently charred to destroy the look of newness before they are used. The choice of the most natural and unobtrusive colors and surfaces point up the qualities of *wabi* and *sabi*. The two words imply a discriminating taste for simplicity and refined rusticity.

Jimi, Hade, and Iki

In addition to *shibui* which is the essence of Japanese culture and considered the ultimate in taste, there are three other kinds of Japanese beauty: *jimi, hade* and *iki*.

Jimi means sober and sedate, unobtrusive, properly correct but dull, and obvious without character. Most Japanese strive for *shibui* but many fall short of the goal and achieve only *jimi*. *Shibui* requires more depth of understanding and subtleness.

Hade, bright colors and bold patterns, has youthful exhuberance. In tourist publicity this is the face Japan puts on for the world. It is typified by the *kimono* of young women and *geisha*.

Iki means stylish, clever and sophisticated. This is the Japanese equivalent to the French word *chic*.

FLOWERS, GARDENS, ZEN AND TEA CULT

II

Flower arrangement, gardens and the tea cult have an inseparable relationship, for they are born of the same spirit. The spiritual meaning of these, as well as dozens of other refinements found in Japanese culture, is based upon the philosophic enlightenment of Buddhism. The Zen Buddhist sect which came to Japan from China in the thirteenth century has had inestimable control over the Oriental mind and artistic work, especially the garden, flower arrangement, and tea ceremony.

All arts are so intimately associated with religion that we cannot have a true understanding of any art or of the people who create it, if we are totally ignorant of the faith of the people. The religion of the Japanese is so unlike ours of the Western world as to seem altogether complicated and confusing. Although I always avoid discussions of religion (and politics), I feel that Japanese gardens and flower arrangement cannot be really understood and appreciated without some knowledge of Japan's religious and social evolution and the forces which shaped and tempered the character of the people.

Until recent years writings on Japanese religion were chiefly by people wholly intolerant of that religion, and lacking in real understanding. Now many excellent books can be purchased in readable, nontechnical language that will give insight into a culture founded on the idea of man in harmonious relationship with nature—a philosophy that has resulted in a national taste of refined simplicity.

Shinto and Buddhism

Shinto, the aboriginal Japanese faith of ancestor worship, held the belief that spirits (*kami*) inhabit all animate and many inanimate objects. This led the

17

Japanese to approach life with reverence, since this philosophy means that they are in contact with the divine when they are performing even the most menial task. Thus the artist of primitive Japan could collect no kind of material, no tree or flower could be cut, nothing could be built, not even an oven for firing pottery, without appealing to the *kami* resident in each thing used. There was a religious way to perform even the most routine work. When Buddhism came out of China by way of Korea in the sixth century, bringing with it the broad flood of Chinese culture, it destroyed no native Shinto beliefs but provided more work and higher ideals for Shinto Gods. Today, in many Japanese homes there are both Shinto and Buddhist altars.

The Japanese people of the sixth century were conscious of what they lacked, materially and spiritually. Not only where they eager to learn from the Chinese, the most advanced culture in the world at that time, but they were extremely capable of using their newly acquired knowledge to develop a superb national art of their own. On the first tide of this irresistible flood which covered the land, to fertilize and nourish the arts, came flowers arranged as offerings to Buddha and the creation of gardens as artistic expression of the highest truths. By the eighth century Japan was in full cultural growth. Zen was introduced during the thirteenth century and by the fifteenth century Japanese art had been developed and refined to a remarkable degree, and had a particular salt and flavor that could be nothing but Japanese.

Zen

It would be brash indeed for a foreigner of an entirely different religious background to attempt to explain and define Zen. Even teachers of Zen call it indefinable. Obviously I can present only partial and broken truths. However there is something to be said for the remarks of a sympathetic outsider.

The illusive and mystic doctrine of Zen cannot be transmitted in writing or through ritual or visual means. There are no scripture, images, ceremonies or formal program of spiritual development. The masters do not instruct by lecture or sermons, but only hint and indicate and put the student through apparently soulless discipline as he strives, through meditation, to achieve *satori* (enlightenment) or the perception of reality. The instructor covertly watches over every act of the student as he goes about given tasks in the monastery, field,

4. (*Opposite*) *A Zen garden. It is quite an art to shape sanded areas with a heavy rake, and usually the design is severely simple but occasionally it is more complicated. Wide circles symbolize raindrops falling on a pond.*

and garden. Speed, skill and taste are noted, but of more importance are willingness, zeal, conscientiousness, unselfishness and service to others.

The method of the Zen teacher is to exhaust the will and the intellect, and at the same time excite, puzzle and baffle. The seeker is brought out of all intellectual pretension and his imagination challenged. He has to learn to *concentrate* in order to *meditate*. This demands the capacity to think of the same thing for hours or days or weeks on end as he sits in what is called Zasen (sitting Zen), a Buddhalike fashion.

In his search for ultimate Truth and realization of the oneness of all creation, sitting in solitary mediation is not enough. The training of the Zen priest includes intellectual drill in the form of seemingly simple or elaborately unsolvable questons (*kòans*) which are given him to ponder. The koan permits no lazy daydreaming and requires a supreme mental effort. Here are examples:

> If you meet someone on the street who has attained the Absolute, you must pass him, neither speaking nor in silence. How would you meet him?

> A Zen Master held one hand in the air and told the pupils to listen to the sound it made. What was the sound?

When such questions apparently have simple answers, the seemingly obvious solution will more than likely be proved wrong by the teacher. If, on the other hand, an elaborate philosophical solution is offered by the seeker, the master may insist on a practical answer. Thus the master guides the pupil toward the realization of the Absolute. He learns that Truth can be in one sense verifiable facts, and in another sense abstract truth.

Sometimes the master sees that his pupil is on the verge of *satori* and knows that prolonged reflection will not reveal the solution. He knows that only a sudden shock will bring the realization of supreme wisdom, whereupon, the master twists his pupil's nose or kicks him from the room. Only at the moment of acute pain, which stopped him from *thinking*, did he find the solution through satori, enlightenment.

SATORI Satori comes like a flash of lightning. It speaks directly to the meditator but only when he realizes that the Buddha is in his own heart and in all nature as well. The vision that comes to the seeker is sudden and is so physically clear that it brings with it absolute certainty in a way that he instantly *sees* and *understands* that things *are* by virtue of what they are *not,* and they owe their being to the not-being of the source of origin. He has an insight into the very nature of things. What has happened? The pupil has not found any new interpretation or new thought. Actually, in a flash of enlightenment, he has come to the answer as if a new third eye, a spiritual eye, had been given him. Things he sees are no different from before, he just sees them differently. His vision as well as perhaps he himself has changed. "The finger pointing at the moon is not the moon itself."

From this seeming confusion and the long periods of inner process the inner image finally unfolds. This is also the way into art.

Followers of Zen Buddhism have produced some of the most artistic gardens of all times, which have exerted vital influence on the art of gardens of the East. They have contributed equally to the art of flower arranging. One would think that there would be no room for expressing one's personality by people trained in such strict channels of behavior as Zen priests, yet they have given us works of great spontaneity. These artists did not create nature as it actually is, no more than a poet writes from nature. Their works have great abstraction and symbolism of a spiritual nature. In creating these masterpieces, the Zen artist applies the principle of *muga* ("it is not I that am doing this"). This is said to open the gate for essential truth to flow in, and when the self does not control creative expression, meaning must.

> Buddha's answer to:
>> "Where is truth?"
>>> "Where truth is self is not.
>>> Where self is truth is not."

The founder of the doctrine of Zen is reputed to be a Buddhist priest of India, Daruma, or Bodhidharma. Figures of him are the most popular of all deities in Japan. Japanese children pay unwitting homage to Zen because one of their favorite toys on sale in every toy shop is the Daruma, a round, red doll that is legless because Daruma, the sage, is said to have sat in meditation for nine long years until he lost the use of his legs. In these nine years of meditation he evolved a doctrine of Dhyama or Zen. The word Zen is derived from the Sanscrit "dhyana" meaning meditation.

The Daruma doll has no legs but is made with weights in it that will immediately return it to an upright position every time it is knocked down. This symbolizes an undaunted spirit. *Nanakorobi-yaoki*, a phrase credited to Daruma, means "seven falls and eight rises" indicating an undaunted spirit. One may fail seven times but will succeed on the eighth attempt so long as one has the understanding spirit.

Zen today still enjoys a certain amount of prestige among educated Japanese. An interesting phenomena of the last twenty-five years has been a rapid and widespread interest in Zen in the West. Even people who have never read about Zen are profoundly impressed by its spirit of restraint, its emphasis on contemplation, its sereneness and its distaste for ritual and dogma, as well the many beautiful things of an artistic nature it has brought in its wake. The enduring and universal attraction of the Japanese garden with its idealized artistic clarity, simplicity, warmth and faithfulness to nature's ways are the work not of professional designers but of Zen priests and cultured laymen. In the same spirit, they have perfected ikebana to the aesthetic expression that it came to be.

The scriptures of Zen could be symbolized with the characters of heaven, man and earth, as portrayed in flower arrangement.

The aim of Zen training is to overcome the trials and worries of the world and attain peace of mind and strength of character. This is the aim of all religions.

In my friendships with people of many lands and religions I have come to feel that in spite of multitudes of differences, basically and simply all of us—Buddhist, Hindu, Moslem, Jew and Christian—are striving to reach the same lofty mountaintop; only our roads are different. When we have respect for one another's faith and keep our hearts and minds open, we may find that the roads are not really as different as at first they appear. I know that my study of Zen has made me a better Christian.

Tea

The tea plant was known from very early times by the Chinese and was highly prized for medicinal purposes. It was believed to have great healing powers and to be good for relieving fatigue, strengthening the will and enlightening the soul with its flavor and aroma. Chinese Taoists considered it an elixir of immortality and Zen Buddhists used it to prevent drowsiness during their long meditations and vigils.

When a Zen monk achieves *satori,* enlightenment, the fact is often transmitted to his master by the way he drinks his tea. The state of mental relaxedness which results from *satori* brings about a profound inner transformation reflected in a relaxedness of the body. He drinks his tea in such a way that he no longer knows whether he is the drinker or the drink, completely forgetful of himself and lost to himself. The drinker is one with the drink; the drink is one with the drinker.

Poets eulogized tea calling it "the froth of the liquid jade."

The earliest records of tea drinking in Japan is the year 729 when one hundred Buddhist monks were invited to the Imperial palace in Nara for tea. Tea at this time was probably one of the most precious commodities brought from China, because it was not until 805 that seeds were reportedly first planted in Japan.

THE TEA CEREMONY

The tea cult, *cha-no-yu,* is a secular ritual indigenous to Japan. Of the many significant avenues of approach open to those interested in the cultural life of

5. *Young ladies learning the tea ceremony at Omote-Senke School in Kyoto.*

the Japanese, nothing is more closely associated with flower arranging and gardens and other arts and crafts than the tea ceremony. It is said that to understand and appreciate the beauty and discipline of the tea ceremony is to know the true Japan. By turning to an art which is so strongly influenced by Zen perhaps we can also gain a better insight into the mysticism of Zen itself.

Tea ceremony, gardens and flower arrangement are so closely wedded to Zen that they are often said to be the result of Zen. They should not, however, be considered parasites of Zen. The same climate and soil have, since about the fourteenth century, nourished equally the tenets of Zen and the symbolism and development in flower arrangement, gardens and later the cult of tea.

The tea ceremony was originally a monastic custom introduced into Japan by Japanese Buddhists who had gone to China to study. Zen monks formed the

23

custom of gathering before the image of Bodhidharma and drinking tea from a single bowl with the profound formality of a holy sacrament. It was from these religious rituals that the tea ceremony was eventually developed into a restrained and rigorous aesthetic cult which has exerted unbelievable force on innumerable facets of Japanese culture since its introduction in the fifteenth century. It has thoroughly flavored the life and tastes of the nation. The most significant thing about the cult and practice of tea is that no other custom in Japan can illustrate so perfectly the sensitive side of Japanese nature and no other force, except Zen which developed it, has been so powerful in inculcating simplicity and restraint, the ingredients of their discriminating taste. Through the tea ceremony, flower arrangement and gardens the Japanese acquired a taste for a refined simplicity aimed at harmonious human relations.

The fundamentals of Zen philosophy as applied to tea ceremony are *Wa-Kei-Sei-Jaku,* Harmony, Respect, Purity and Tranquility. The tea ceremony is an extension of Zen philosophy to the sphere of social gathering and includes both the garden and flower arrangement in its performance.

The Tea Master Rikyu

Many great tea masters helped to formulate the rules for Cha-no-yu, but the greatest of them all was Sen-no-Soeki, 1521-1591, who was better known by his court name Rikyu. Rikyu was not only famous as a tea master but noted also as a master designer of gardens and flower arrangements and as an undoubted arbiter of styles, social etiquette and taste.

He was chosen by the great General Hideyoshi to revise the rules of Cha-no-yu and purge it from extravagances and excesses which had crept in. Under the patronage of Hideyoshi he refined the tea ceremony and raised it to the dignity of a national art. Rikyu laid down strict rules concerning the etiquette of the tea ceremony and prescribed principles that called for utter simplicity in all things related to the tea ceremony. He insisted that the tea utensils should never be ostentatious or of costly material. When the fashion grew for antiques to be used in serving tea, he counseled against extreme rarity and high cost of such things. These rules still constitute the basic principles as taught by all the schools that came after. Of all the strict rules Rikyu formulated for the tea ceremony perhaps the most rigid was that among gentlemen there must be no rigidity!

Scores of stories are told about Rikyu to illustrate the delicacy and discrimination of the tea ceremony. After many years spent in its refinement, Rikyu once said, "There is no secret in the art of Cha-no-yu. You first boil the water, then fuse the tea, and then drink it according to traditional rules." When someone replied, "I know how to do all this," the great Master of tea answered, "If there really is someone who knows how, I will become his pupil!"

Rikyu at one time went with his son to visit another tea master and admire his garden. The son was much impressed with a moss-covered gate that opened into the inner garden, but Rikyu said, "I don't agree. That gate must have been brought from a distant mountain temple at obvious expense. A rustic one made by a local carpenter would give the place the appropriate quiet and lonely look, and not offend us by bringing up thoughts of difficulty and expense. I doubt that we shall find here a sensitive or interesting tea ceremony."

Another time after watching his son sweep and clean the tea garden until it was scrupulously clean he expressed dissatisfaction with the appearance of the garden. To his son's bewilderment he walked over to a tree that grew by the side of the path and shook it, scattering autumn leaves over the freshly raked and washed stones. He instructed his son by saying, "A garden must not appear too strictly groomed, but must have natural beauty. The falling leaves express the spirit of nature and the mood of the season."

Rikyu is credited with originating the Nageire style of flower arrangement and making it a part of the tea ceremony. Rikyu was on the battlefield with the great General Hideyoshi one hot day, so the story goes, when the opposing armies paused, by mutual consent, so that their generals could enjoy a cup of tea. General Hideyoshi asked Rikyu to arrange some iris which were growing nearby. The tea master picked the iris, grouping a few leaves around them. Then piercing the stems with the blade of his dagger, he tossed the group into a waterbucket, which had been placed near the general in a crude attempt at air-conditioning. The arrangement stood upright in the bucket and the general, impressed with its design cried, "What a beautiful throw-in arrangement!" Thus the Nageire style flower arrangement became a part of the tea ceremony.

It might be supposed that the military growth of a nation would mean the suppression of the arts, but this was not the case. The military men, faced with the task of administering the laws as well as guarding the country, felt the need for a simple form of religion, practical for camp life yet profound enough to inspire and give vigor to the mind. Zen Buddhism with its simple and practical qualities met this need. Zen appealed to the temper and ideals of war lords and feudal warriors because it did not depend on scriptures, the worship of idols or ceremonies, but each believer must work out his own salvation through austere mental discipline and meditation. Poise and peace of mind, particularly useful during difficult times, was attained through a moral life founded on spiritual training associated with the aesthetic refinement so much a part of Zen. The combination of moral life and the sense of beauty was the basis of *Bushido*, the way of the warrior.

The most famous story of all concerning Rikyu is that of his final tea ceremony. A rift occurred between him and General Hideyoshi and he had been

6. A drawing of a Japanese tea house from an old book on Japanese gardens.

condemned to die. Rikyu asked and was granted the favor of being allowed to officiate at a final tea ceremony. Rikyu appeared calm and poised as he received his guests. In the room hung a kakemono which symbolized the "passing of all earthly things." Each guest was presented with an object of art or a tea ceremony implement. At the end of the ceremony Rikyu took the cup from which he had drunk and broke it into fragments as a symbol that his cup of misfortune should not be passed to another. Thus ended the final tea ceremony of the greatest master of all, Sen-no-Rikyu. After the departure of his guests he removed his outer garments revealing the pure white robes of death, and drawing his dagger he performed the solemn and dignified ceremony of taking his own life. Thus he redeemed his honor.

Tea House

The tea house, like the tea ceremony itself, reflects the aesthetic ideals and teachings of Zen Buddhism. The architecture is that of a simple country farmhouse with a thatched roof and suggests refined poverty. The rooms usually consist of a waiting room, the tea room and an anteroom or pantry where tea utensils are washed and stored. Though a tea house has the appearance of poverty they are built carefully of the choicest materials. They may cost more per square foot than an expensive dwelling or even a temple.

Room sizes in Japan are measured by multiples of tatami mats that cover the floor. The conventional size of the tea room proper of a tea house is four and one-half mats which in our measurement is between nine and ten feet square. However, sizes may vary from the smallest tea rooms which are one and one-half mats in size to very large ones of sometimes twelve mats. The waiting room is usually three tatamis in size.

In a wealthy home a particular room of the main dwelling is often set aside for the tea ceremony, taking the place of the tea house. The very early tea room, in fact, consisted of merely partitioning off with screens a portion of a large room.

The only entrance for a traditional tea room from the outside is through a small opening usually about two feet by two and one-half feet. It is purposely low so that the guests have to creep through. This is to inculcate humility because as one enters he must leave behind worldly power and possessions. Another feature of the tea house is a small tokonoma (average size of which is four feet by two feet) in which is displayed a picture scroll and flower arrangement.

The interior is designed to accommodate no more than five guests. A hearth is usually built into the floor on which is placed an iron kettle. The walls are of plaster and are a soft restful beige tone to induce a mood of tranquility and contemplation. Mellowness of age is suggested by the soft coloring and somber light which is subdued and diffused as it comes in through small windows with grills of bamboo and *shoji* or sliding panels covered with rice paper.

7. (Above) A charming tea house by a pond in a large Japanese garden.

8. (Below) Elegant simplicity is the keynote of a tea garden. This drawing shows the layout of a garden which includes a yoritsuki (waiting room), roji (dewy path), tsukubai (purification basin), and stone lantern.

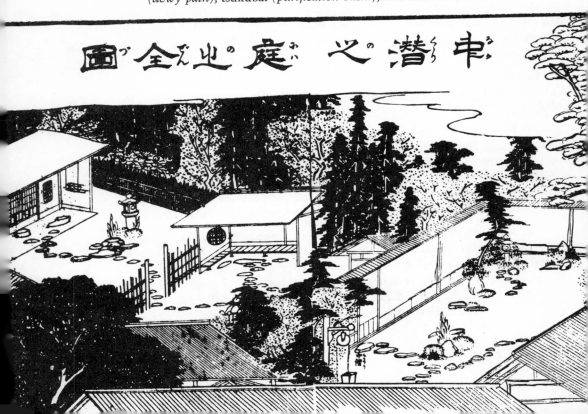

中くぐりの潜り庭にの止と全ぜん園づ図

The tea room in its design and material, like the garden and tea ceremony itself, suggests the qualities *wabi* and *sabi,* as prescribed by the tea master Rikyu. *Wabi* can be translated as gracefulness, tranquility, rusticity and harmonious though unbalanced beauty. *Sabi,* a more abstract quality, means unobtrusive and patinated by use and age. *Wabi* and *sabi* imply a discriminating taste for simplicity and rusticity.

The Tea Garden

Tea masters with their Zen Buddhist cast of mind have made the most valuable contribution to the gardens of Japan. Like the tea house the tea garden reflects their philosophies. The formal tea garden follows certain prescribed rules for the proper performance of the tea ceremony. To the sensitive Japanese the setting must have an appropriate atmosphere in every respect in order to induce the correct spiritual attitude.

The classical tea gardens were usually divided into three parts. The outer or entrance garden is very small and simple. A short walk leads into the middle garden. In the middle garden is the waiting area near which is a thatch-covered bench where arriving guests wait for the host to come out and greet them. From the bench a garden path called a *roji* leads to the tea house or tea room. This is of irregularly laid stepping stones and is the most important part of the tea garden. Great care is lavished on this area and many arts employed to suggest the woods or a mountain path. One may be in the midst of a great city and yet feel as if in a distant forest. The *roji* was intended to break connection with the outside world, bring about a mood of calm withdrawal from earthly cares and cleanse the spirit. Before entering the tea house a guest must pause and meditate and prepare himself spiritually for the tea ceremony.

The inner tea garden, seen from the tea room itself, is a small enclosed area. Near the tea house is a stone water basin called *tsukubai* from a similar Japanese word which means to crouch, because one must bend over to use the water in the basin. Here guests observe the ritual of washing their hands and rinsing their mouth before entering the ceremony room. This signifies the washing away of the cares and sins of the world. Close by the water basin always stands a stone lantern which is lighted by a candle for an evening tea ceremony. The best height for this lantern is about five feet, and it should be simple and dignified, never overly carved or ornamented. There is sometimes a bench near the tea house much like that in the middle garden. It is provided as a place for guests to rest between the first and second sessions of a formal tea ceremony.

Ritual Tea Ceremony

There are a number of ways of conducting the tea ceremony, *cha-no-yu,* depending on the occasion, season, precepts of school being followed and the type of tea served. The hour of the day for holding a tea ceremony also varies depending on the season and occasion. In a formal tea ceremony a host entertains his guests first with a light meal called *kaiseki* followed by a thick, pasty, green tea called *koicha,* and last a foamy tea brew known as *usucha.* The whole procedure requires about four hours. Sometimes only the foamy tea, *usucha,* is served. For this informal style only about one hour is required.

When a formal *cha-no-yu* is given, invitations are sent out a week or more in advance, either in person or in writing, usually to five people (a number that can be served in a traditional-size tea room). Etiquette demands that the guests respond promptly to the invitation and those accepting will call on the host the day before the party to express their thanks in advance.

FORMAL CHA-NO-YU   Following is a general description of the formal serving and drinking of ceremonial tea:

1. The host prepares for the party. He gives special thought to the flower arrangement and the *kakemono* or hanging scroll to be placed in the *tokonoma,* the ornaments suitable for the occasion and the food. Just before time for the party he sweeps the garden and its path and sprinkles it with water, and arranges the tea utensils in proper order.

2. The guests arrive about fifteen minutes before the appointed time and assemble in the garden or in the small waiting room, *yoritsuki,* where they prepare for the tea. By strict *cha-no-yu* etiquette a ring, wrist-watch or any jewelry that could possibly damage the tea bowl or other valuable utensils should be removed. No perfume should be worn. This would contaminate the pure aroma of the tea and spoil the fragrance of ceremonial incense which is often used. Clothes of quiet colors in keeping with the simplicity and calmness, which are the essential requirement of a *cha-no-yu* party, should be worn. No *haori* (short overgarment) is worn inside the tea room. Footgear must be removed before stepping up into the room. Guests should have with them at the tea party: a small folding fan; a pad of *kaishi,* or small pieces of white paper on which to place the cake and for use in wiping the fingers; and one or two pieces of silk called *fukusa,* usually red or purple in color, folded double in about ten-inch squares. The *fukusa* is placed under the tea bowl and other articles the guest takes in his hand to admire. These with other necessities are carried in a special case. When the guests are assembled and ready in the waiting room, an assistant to the host usually appears at the entrance, bows, prepares a cup of hot water for each guest to drink, and invites them into the garden where there is a wooden bench or arbor. Special straw sandals are provided for this.

3. The host comes out into the garden and welcomes his guests with a bow. The guests stand up and bow and proceed slowly toward the tea room down

9. *The stone water basin where guests at a tea ceremony wash away worldly thoughts.*

the *roji* or meaningful garden path. They go in single file with the principal guest leading. The leader is usually a person well posted in the art who has been chosen by the host in advance; however, the guests sometimes arrange this between themselves while waiting in the *yoritsuki*. The leader, as guest of honor, acts as spokesman and retains this responsibility throughout the ceremony.

4. Close to the tea room is a stone water basin, *tsukubai*, beside a stone lantern. Here guests pause and each in turn performs the ritual of washing his hands and rinsing his mouth. The slow walk along the garden path, *roji*, and the purification ceremony at the water basin are intended to prepare

the guest for the strict spiritual discipline which reigns throughout a true *cha-no-yu.*

5. Guests leave their sandals at the steps and creep through the small, low opening one by one. In proper order each guest in turn kneels in front of the *tokonoma* or alcove and placing his fan in front of him makes a respectful obeisance. He then admires in turn the hanging scroll and the flower arrangement. On the shelf there may be two or three other art objects tastefully displayed among them a tiny incense burner. These are also admired. Next he looks at the kettle and hearth with respectful attention after which he takes his proper place according to tea ceremony rules with the principal guest seated before the *tokonoma.*

6. The host makes his appearance from the pantry. The leader and other guests greet the host politely and thank him for his invitation. As spokesman for the group, the leader, inquires about the garden, the *kakemono* that hangs in the *tokonoma* and the flower arrangement and expresses his admiration of those works of art, and other objects chosen for their enjoyment.

7. For the first session of a formal tea ceremony a light repast called *kaiseki* is served. This consists of a few dishes carefully prepared and served with great formality and in fixed order by the host. Since the food is served in small quantities and is lightly flavored it is rude not to eat everything. The host does not eat with his guests but in a separate room. This is a sign of respect for the guest as is the fact that the host has also prepared and served the food himself. A clever host will make the time pass pleasantly by telling an entertaining incident or story each time he comes out to serve.

8. When the light repast is over the guests retire again to the bench in the garden for a short recess.

9. The host sounds a gong, usually five or seven soft strokes, as a signal for guests to return to the tea house for the second session which is the true ceremony of tea. The guests repeat the purification formality at the basin and enter the tea room in the same order as before. They again kneel before the *tokonoma* and admire the flower arrangement. There is no longer a *kakemono* for in the cult of thick powdered tea, *koicha,* there is a rule not to have at the same time a hanging scroll and flower arrangement in the alcove.

10. The host now by following precise rules and ritual prepares and serves *koicha,* a thick pasty green tea, made from the powdered young leaves of old tea plants that are from twenty to seventy years old. It resembles very thick spinach soup in consistency and in color. This is whipped to a creamy froth with a split bamboo whisk. Tea for several guests is made in one big bowl using two or three spoonfulls of tea and enough water for three and one-half mouthfuls for each person. The bowl is placed first in front of the

head guest who receives it with ceremonious gestures, drinks and passes the bowl to the next person.

TO DRINK KOICHA   The proper way to drink thick green tea is to hold the tea bowl on a *fukusa* (doubled silk cloth) in the palm of the left hand supporting one side with the right hand. After nodding to the next guest saying, *Osaki-ni*, "Before you," turn the bowl to the left, bringing the side without the design to the front and take about three sips. Wipe the edge of the bowl where lips touched with a piece of paper, *kaishi*, and pass the bowl to the next guest. After all guests have partaken of the tea in the same manner the last guest hands the bowl back to the host, who after washing it and going through more prescribed formalities, passes the empty bowl to the first guest. Each guest in turn admires the bowl, tea caddy, dipper and other utensils. The leader, on behalf of the others, inquires about their origin and history. Looking at each article carefully and with interest is good etiquette. The custom of handing around the loving-cup, still prevalent in England, offers an interesting analogy to the Japanese way of drinking thick, powdered green tea from a common bowl. The ceremony also resembles the sacrament of Holy Communion in which the communicants drink from a common cup.

11. The succeeding and final part of the *cha-no-yu* party is the serving of *usucha,* a frothy green tea made of powdered young tea leaves from young tea plants that are from three to fifteen years old. The serving of *usucha* along with sweet-meats forms the only course of the informal *cha-no-yu* party.

Before preparing *usucha* the fire is carefully examined and replenished. The same utmost exactness and systematized performance and long formalities are required for *usucha* as for *koicha.* For this course sometimes cushions and tobacco trays are brought in. The tea is so timed that it will be ready for each guest while he is eating his cake. Since the cake is eaten first, it is best to start eating just when the host begins preparing the tea. The cake is taken from the tray with chopsticks, if they are provided, or with the fingers. The principal guest takes a cake first and places it on a piece of paper, *kaishi,* before him on the tatami mat. The others follow suit each making an apology to the person next to him as a matter of form. The tea is prepared for each guest one at a time and in separate bowls.

TO DRINK USUCHA   As soon as the tea is set before you, bow to the person whose turn will be next as an apology for taking the privilege of precedence, lift the bowl onto the palm of the left hand protecting it with the right, raise the bowl up almost level with the forehead then lower it a little. Next put the right hand on the edge of the bowl and turn it a little. (Each school has its own way of turning the bowl.) The idea is that since the host has set the bowl before you with what he considers most important part facing you it should be turned a little to avoid putting the lips on that particular part. All the tea should be drunk to the very last drop. When finished the part of the bowl touched by the lips is wiped lightly with the fingers of the right hand and then the fingers wiped with *kaishi,* pocket paper. The bowl is now placed on the mat in the position the host placed it and then lifted again in both hands and its beauty and interest admired. It is scrutinized closely and turned upside down for inspection, but very carefully and never should it be held high or carelessly. The bowl is then returned to the host.

When all the guests have finished their tea they take turns admiring the tea caddy and the tea spoon. They look first at each object with their hands on the mat and then take it carefully in both hands for a closer look. It is customary for the principal guest to ask, on behalf of the others, questions about these art objects. After a great deal of prescribed formality concerning the tea utensils the host makes a silent bow to denote the ceremony is finished. Guests then proceed to the waiting room where they prepare to go home.

12. After three or four days a guest must not fail to write a note of thanks or call in person at the host's home to express thanks.

INFORMAL CHA-NO-YU   At the informal tea ceremony all the formalities listed above are observed but no repast or thick green tea are served. In other words, the general procedure outlined above may be followed except that steps 7, 8, 9 and 10 are omitted. It is to the informal tea ceremony that foreign lovers of Japanese culture are usually invited. Few are ever invited to the full formal ritual.

Apart from typical *usucha* or foamy green tea ceremony are numerous other ways of serving ceremonial tea. I have outlined in general the traditional procedures, but these may be modified to suit certain situations. Very often *cha-no-yu* is served quite informally without sending out a formal invitation and a meal may or may not be served. A large room is sometimes used for entertaining many guests at one time. A garden party is at times planned where dozens of people are entertained with tea served in different pavilions and *cha-no-yu* can be appreciated in the bosom of nature.

Due to Western influences there has been a tendency in a few areas to introduce tables and chairs for the comfort of foreigners and to adapt tea ceremony to Western style rooms and to Western dress. One tea master of great taste has been giving lessons in *cha-no-yu* to American ladies and has reportedly been highly successful in adapting tea ceremony to the Western way of living.

Unfortunately many visitors to Japan experience only tea ceremonies that are staged as tourist attractions. The serving of tea so practiced is frozen into meaningless correctness and is more like a side show depicting a polite but dull pastime than a true *cha-no-yu*.

I have said little about the art of conducting the tea ceremony. Those who practice *cho-no-yu* follow a regulated mode of serving with utensils carefully selected and correctly arranged. Utmost exactness in handling the tea implements is demanded and not a single error must occur in the performance of the function. The accuracy and grace of each act teaches precision, poise, tranquility, courtesy, sincerity and grace.

Training in the serving and drinking of ceremonial tea includes nearly all phases of etiquette observed in Japanese living. For this reason young ladies take lessons in tea ceremony to learn correct manners and deportment. They often practice the art of flower arrangement and the etiquette of ceremonial tea in the morning and go to dancing school in the afternoon.

Anyone without previous experience need not be perturbed by the rigid rules of etiquette when invited to attend a tea ceremony. Japanese friends are always happy to tell you what to do and what not to do and guide you through the formalities. You should not hesitate to ask for directions whenever puzzled at any stage of the ceremony. Though the procedure seems confusing and precise it need not worry you. Wear something neat and simple and take things as they come. When you see something beautiful, say it is beautiful; when doing something before someone else excuse yourself with *Osaki-ni* or "Before you"; and do everything in an orderly, reserved and calm manner. If you have a sincere, simple and modest attitude you will be in tune to the occasion, for these feelings are an integral part of the cult of tea.

Powdered green tea is usually associated with the tea ceremony, but powdered tea is not always used. A very high grade leaf tea was used at the most charming and meaningful tea ceremony I have witnessed. This was in Tokyo at the home of Mr. Choca Adachi, Headmaster of the Adachi School of Flower Arrangement. The ceremony was so gracefully and naturally conducted and our hearts and spirits were in such complete harmony that we were well into the formalities before I realized we were participating in a genuine *cha-no-yu*. It seemed fitting that we should discuss the state of the fire and the beautiful ancient kettle as we listened to "the soughing wind in the pines," the music it made as the water boiled. Without knowing it was the correct thing to do I asked about the priceless bowls from which we drank our tea. Mr. Adachi brought out other objects of art for our enjoyment, among them his famous scrolls of "One Hundred Camellias."

Mr. Adachi called the tea *sen-cha* and spoke of its rarity. He made the brew in a large bowl and then divided it into small bowls for serving. The temperature of the water for this tea is very important, he explained. First it must "boil completely," then cool to just the right degree. (Water too hot will spoil fine tea.)

Water was boiled, cooled, poured over the tea leaves and served three times. "The first time for aroma, second time for color and the third time for flavor," Mr. Adachi explained.

As we took our leave of Mr. Adachi, his wife and beautiful daughter, we knew we had experienced something precious and unforgettable. In beautifully simple and serene surroundings, through conforming to the gentle rigors of Zen and tea, we had enjoyed a calm withdrawal from worldly cares. With a kindred spirit we had discussed tea, camellias and flower arrangement. Our host had shared with us the beauty of his home, garden, art treasures and the cult of tea.

Such experiences are too few. More participation in the gentle arts of flowers, gardens and tea can ease the hurry and worry of our machine and space age and help us achieve a serene mind and calm spirit. As one of our Western poets expressed it, we may be able:

> "To see a world in a grain of sand
> And a Heaven in a wild flower,
> Hold Infinity in the palm of your hand
> And Eternity in an hour."

10. *The Silver Pavilion, Ginkakuji, significantly related to the history of flower arrangements, Japanese gardens, and the development of the tea and incense ceremonies, as seen through the branches of an ancient pine tree. Note the limb support.*

INCENSE CEREMONY

The Incense ceremony *(kodo)*, the art of flower arrangement *(ikebana)*, and the tea ceremony *(cha-no-yu)* formed an ancient triad which was regarded as an institution of cultural enlightenment and mental and spiritual tranquility. All three are characteristically Japanese and each contributed to the strict observance of ceremony and highly developed sense of courteous behavior. The refined sense of smell developed by incense burning is believed to cultivate mental composure in the same way that flower arrangement and the tea ceremony cultivate mental and physical poise.

It is not known exactly when the incense ceremony evolved as a fully constituted secular ritual, but in the fifteenth century it had acquired the form of an aesthetic pastime known as *ko-kwai* or incense party. It made great advancement under the patronage of the Shogun Ashikaga Yoshimasa (Shogun from 1443-73), who was a patron also of the arts of landscape gardening, tea ceremony and flower arrangement. Adjacent to Yoshimasa's Silver Pavilion (Ginkakugi) in Kyoto is a small, beautiful building, the Togudo, which contains two rooms called the *roseitei*. These are reproductions of those used by Yoshimasa for incense parties. In the same building is the famous tea room designed by Shuko, a Zen monk. This points up the fact that incense parties apparently enjoyed the same widespread popularity as the tea ceremony.

At first the incense ceremony was a pastime of the aristocracy exclusively but later cultured members of the wealthy merchant class became devotees. It still has its votaries among the upper clases in Japan.

History of Incense in Japan

Incense burning has been associated with Buddhism for centuries and it is generally accepted that incense was brought into Japan by Buddhist priests in the sixth century. These were the same priests who introduced the custom of arranging flowers as offerings to Buddha.

The burning of incense was employed by the Hindus in worshipping their gods and cremating the dead from remote antiquity. It was natural that it should become a part of Buddhist worship in India and then spread with the religion to Japan by way of China and Korea.

Incense burning is an impressive part of Buddhist religious ceremonies in Japan today. The presence of many worshippers around large incense burners at Buddhist temples always intrigues me.

Gradually in the centuries after its introduction incense came to be used for secular and recreational uses as well as for religious worship. In the secular sense it began to be used about the fifteenth century for scenting rooms when guests were expected and for perfuming clothing. In feudal times warriors perfumed their helmets with incense before going into battle. Thus they maintained the etiquette of polite society even on the field of battle providing, if they should be killed, that their bodies would be sweet smelling.

There are many different kinds of incense and considerable variations in quality. Often the perceptible difference between the best blends are extremely subtle and to guess the nature and name of a compound from the perfume of its smoke one must be endowed with very acute and cultivated olfactory powers. The foundation of incense in Japan from the tenth century until the present is *awaseko,* mixed incense. The many substances used to make the various varieties are obtained from odorous woods, roots, barks, dried flowers, seeds, fruits, herbs and gum resins. The ancient buyer of incense acquired the habit of sampling different blends to get the type he preferred. It is thought that the custom of selecting one's own brand led to the meeting of friends to test their sense of smell which in time developed into organized competition for guessing different incense.

The Incense Ceremony

The incense ceremony, like the tea ceremony, is a social affair conducted according to prescribed etiquette in a quiet and simple atmosphere. It requires deep concentration and is a highly moral and esthetic form of entertainment. The fundamental principle of the ceremony is guessing the name and nature of each incense as rare incenses are burned. There are many different ways of playing the game, each with its own formula. Sometimes the participants are divided into two teams, the groups making the greatest number of correct guesses winning the prizes. In olden days nobles presented swords, armor and many other valuable treasures to the winners of these competitions. Strict conventions and intricate rules are observed by participants of the ceremony. The host or master of ceremony must be one well versed in the ritual.

The room used is usually of eight mats in size, about twelve by twelve feet. There is always a *tokonoma* with an arrangement of flowers in the room and great care goes into choosing the flowers. The arrangement must not contain any flowers or plant material with a scent as the air must be kept free from any possible conflicting odor. The host sits in the corner opposite the *tokonoma* to greet his guests who take their places in front of the *tokonoma.*

Exquisite utensils are used in the incense ceremony and many of these are treasured collectors' items. Lacquered cabinets used for holding the implements and incense burners, *koro,* are particularly desirable pieces.

Many people of the Western world who are exposed to oriental incense fall under its spell and use its enticing aroma to add charm and interest to their surroundings. Choosing a favorite incense can be more fascinating than experimenting with French perfumes. With an enticing incense burning in a beautiful *koro* and a well done Japanese flower arrangement one can convert a trite interior into a place of mystery and charm. Devotees of incense endow it with qualities of "character," "color" and "taste." If when choosing a scent the olfactory response become numbed, try rinsing the mouth with vinegar from time to time! This will restore to a degree sensitivity to odors.

Children love the exotic experience of choosing a favorite scent. To our grandchildren one of the interesting attractions at "Mimi's and Papou's house" is "Burning my very most favoritest incense." I am sure their lives will be richer for having learned to love watching incense smoke curl from a beautiful old *koro* and to enjoy the exquisite experience of burning incense.

SYMBOLISM

The Japanese artist will often represent the whole sky with one stroke of the brush, the landscape designer will portray a distant mountain by the contour of a single clipped shrub, and sometimes a single flower or tree suffices as a symbol of the inner essence of nature. An expression of the infinite aspect of life and essential character and mood of nature is achieved by simplifying its profusion by the eloquent use of an empty space. An appreciation of aesthetic qualities and symbolism is facilitated by a knowledge of myths, legends, and meaning of some of the decorative motifs of Japanese art. The innumerable symbolisms and myths of Japanese art would fill volumes but we can discuss them here in a summary way.

Three fundamental characteristics of the Japanese way of thinking must be kept in mind when studying ikebana and the art of gardening: an inate love of nature in all its manifestations, a love of line in all forms of artistic expression and an instinctive love of symbolism. The Japanese are not content with the visible forms of nature but search for inner, hidden meanings; for to discover the inner meaning of something far from the obvious gives added pleasure to the viewer. The Japanese are the only people who have chosen so perishable a material as growing, living plants to express their deepest aspirations and emotions. Since ancient times flowers have been as acceptable a medium to the Japanese artist as paints to the European and marble to the Greek.

The Oriental love of line is everywhere manifested even to the roof lines of their houses which are among the most beautiful in the world. Both in the exterior and interior the lines of timber construction are not only unhidden but emphasized. The *torii*, the gate seen before all *Shinto* shrines, is unpretentious and depends solely on line for its beauty but few people having once seen it ever forget the charm of a *torii* silhouetted against the sky. The *torii* symbolically purifies those who pass through. The ideogram for *torii* means bird perch and

11. *The magnificent enclosed garden of Daisen-in, Daitokuji Temple, Kyoto, typifies the dry-landscape style in which mountains, waterfalls, bridges, islands, streams, and sea are represented with sand and rocks of various shapes and sizes.*

specifically alludes to the cave entrance on which a rooster perched in the legendary story of Amaterasu, so most Shinto shrines have three *torii* to represent the three crowings of the rooster.

One of the most important and meaningful traditions from ancient China adapted by the Japanese and surviving today is the Five Colors. The proper sequence of the five cardinal colors is: yellow, blue, red, white and black. Each of the five colors is related in a significant manner to the five seasons of time, five directions, five elements and five virtues. Following are the proper sequences of each to conform to the sequence of color. Seasons of time—*doyo* (each cycle has doyo which is eighteen days at the beginning), spring, summer, autumn, and winter. Five directions—center, east, south, west, and north. Five elements—

12. *The drawing shows rocks in the Zen garden of Daisen-in.*

1. Kogamejima, *baby turtle islet.*

2. Butsubanseki, *Buddha's foot impression stone.*

3. Dokuseiseki, *stone of experience.*

4. Kameshima, *turtle islet. (See inset.)*

5. Kitoseki, *turtle's head stone.*

6. Zazenseki, *stone for Zazen.*

7. Baanseki, *saddle stone.*

8. Fudoseki, *immovable stone.*

9. Kannonishi, *Goddess of mercy's stone.*

10. Horaizen, *Mt. Horai or treasure mountain represented by two clipped camellias.*

11. Taki, *waterfall.*

12. Hossuseki, *priest brush stone.*

13. Chinkoseki, *aloewood stone.*

14. Shiwabuki, *splash of waves.*

15. Horagaiishi, *trumpet shell stone.*

16. Tsurushima, *crane islet. (See inset.)*

17. Darumaishi, *Dharma stone.*

18. Meikyoseki, *bright mirror stone.*

19. Senboseki, *hermit's head stone.*

20. Kotoseki, *tiger's head stone.*

21. Kappaishi, *water imp stone.*

22. Ryotoseki, *dragon's head stone.*

23. Furoseki, *chair stone for the old.*

24. Hakuunseki, *white cloud stone. (Water fairy stone.)*

25. Seki, *dam.*

26. Reikiseki, *turtle stone.*

27. Takara bune, *treasure boat stone.*

28. Eizanseki, *Mt. Hiei stone.*

29. Shinjyuishi, *pearl stone.*

30. Gagyuseki, *sleeping cow stone.*

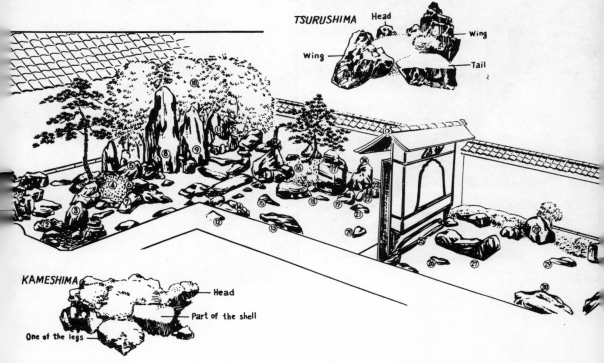

earth, wood, fire, metal, and water. Virtue—faith, humanity, decorum, justice and wisdom. The abstract principles of the symbolism attached to these sets of five Oriental subjects have a profound effect upon all phases of Japanese life.

The zodiacal characters in animal forms are perhaps the most fascinating of all Japanese symbols. They may be used singly or in combination. The solar or Gregorian calendar was adopted in the nineteenth century, but in addition there are two ancient calendars still in use in Japan: the lunar calendar which was introduced along with other things Chinese in the sixth century and the zodiac calendar also of Chinese origin. The farmers still prefer and use the old lunar calendar which they follow in sowing seeds because it tells the climate changes for the seasons better than the solar calendar. The zodiac calendar assigns each year in history and each day of the year a zodiac sign. The years are divided into twelve cycles and each year is named after one of the animals of the twelve Oriental signs of the zodiac. These animals are arranged in the cycle in the following order: rat, ox, tiger, hare, dragon, serpent, horse, sheep, monkey, cock, dog and boar. Correlated with these are the ten trunks making a reciprocal set of zodiac signs so that each year in history and each day of the year has one sign of each set. The ten trunks are an arrangement of the years in cycles of ten each with their names taken from the five elements in the following order: wood senior and junior, fire senior and junior, earth senior and junior, metal senior and junior and water senior and junior.

The Japanese have always lived very close to nature and have a profound appreciation of all its qualities. An emblematic association of certain plants with animals often appears in legends handed down from ancient times. Some plants and animals most frequently combined are dragon and plum blossom, deer and maple, boar and lespedeza, swallow and willow, plover and waves, lion and peony, quail and millet, peacock and peony and cuckoo and wisteria.

Another combination is that of animal-guardian or messenger with respective Shinto deities. The deer, *shika,* is the messenger of the Kasuga shrine in Nara which is dedicated to Takemikazuchi, general in the legendary age of gods. The monkey is the messenger of the Sanno-Sama or Hie shrine in Tokyo dedicated to Oyamakui, an ancient Shinto deity. The dove is consecrated to Hachiman, a god of peace, and every Hachiman shrine has a large number of them. The Inari (rice-bearer) shrine is the most popular of all the Shinto shrines. Hardly a village is without an Inari shrine dedicated to a prehistoric princess called Ugatama-no-Mikoto who according to legend taught the Japanese how to grow

13. *(Opposite) Himeji Castle illustrates the most elaborate of Japanese architecture styles. Note the beautiful lines of roof against the sky.*

rice. Every Inari shrine has a pair of sculptured foxes of stone or wood placed in front as messengers. With the exception of the Inari fox, a good tempered and benevolent creature, foxes are regarded as evil and are reputed to have demoniacal powers. Every area has stories of people said to have been bewitched by foxes.

Another legendary figure with magical powers is *Tanuki* the badger. He is depicted as a mischievous fellow who takes many disguises to deceive and annoy the traveler. He has the reputation of leading people astray in the dark, causing fishermen to draw up their nets empty and laughing at their plight, etc. In the carved or sculptured images of *Tanuki* he is often posed standing by the roadside with a greatly extended stomach and scrotum, wearing a coat of lotus leaves and a lotus flower on his head like a coolie hat and carrying a purse in one hand and a bottle of *sake* in the other.

Especially popular are the *kame,* tortoise and the *tsuru,* crane. Symbols of longevity and good luck they are used in many designs. The crane is usually depicted with pine or bamboo in such characteristic poses as stalking through meadows, perching on pine branches or sweeping aloft in majestic flight. The crane is given the title Patriarch of the Feathered Tribe. It is believed to live several hundred years on water alone, and then when it reaches a thousand years its white plumes turn black. It is held as a model for motherhood because it will stay with its young in time of peril and shield them with its wings in cold weather.

Semba-suru, literally one thousand cranes, is a good luck symbol and is often used in patterns for kimono fabric. The combination *tsurukame,* crane-and-tortoise, implies happiness as well as longevity and good luck. Rocks are often arranged in the garden to represent them. There is a saying that while the crane lives for one thousand years the tortoise lives for ten thousand.

The dragon is another commonly used mythical fauna in Japanese lore. It is one of the Four Sacred Creatures which include the dragon (*ryu*), tortoise (*kame*), unicorn (*kirin*) and phoenix (*ho-o*). Dragons are depicted in many forms. They have the miraculous power of living in the heavens, in the water and on land and may be represented as huge scaly reptiles with sharp claws or winged creatures with horns. Tradition holds that the Imperial sword of Japan was found in the tail of a dragon. The tiger, *tora,* symbol of military prowess and lord of all land animals is frequently associated with the dragon. It represents the wind and the dragon the water. When the two are combined they provide the necessary atmosphere for the sustenance of life. A favorite theme in painting is the scene of a tiger in a bamboo thicket. Since these thickets cannot be invaded by other animals they offer the tiger a refuge from whence his mighty roar makes nature tremble.

The carp, *koi,* is another mythical and symbolic figure. Its greatest use as a symbol is in the boys' festival, *tango-no-sekku,* held each year on the fifth day of the fifth month when huge paper or cloth carp are attached to masts, one for each boy in the household. The symbolic illusion is to the perseverance of the *koi* swimming against the current and attempting to leap waterfalls.

A purely Japanese association is that of the willow and green tree frog because of the story of Ono-no-Dofu, a Japanese nobleman of the tenth century who reached the age of sixty without becoming proficient in calligraphy. One day as he strolled by the river, discouraged by his efforts, he noticed a tiny frog trying to reach a leaf on a hanging branch of willow. The frog tried again and again and on the seventh attempt succeeded. The perseverance of the tiny frog so impressed Ono-no-Dofu that he went home determined not to be less courageous than the lowly frog and applied himself with such vigor that he became one of the greatest calligraphers of his day. Pendant branches of willow

14. *(Left) A classical New Year arrangement of three luck symbols, pine-bamboo-plum.*

15. *(Right) Lotus, the symbol of purity, wisdom and Buddhahood, are often arranged for religious occasions.*

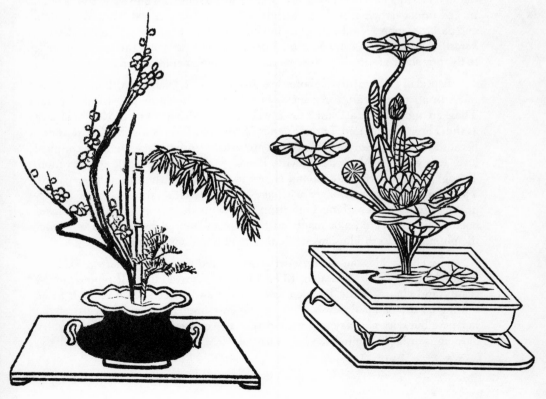

with a frog on the ground beneath is a much used design motif. We often call this type of willow "weeping willow" but it suggests no such idea to the Japanese mind, rather it suggests growth and fresh new life.

The bush warbler, *uguisu,* one of the much loved birds of Japan, is the herald of spring and when used with the plum blossom, *ume,* the two represent spring and happiness. The bush warbler is associated with Buddhism because its flutelike call resembles the name *Ho-hokeyo,* the secret scriptures of a Buddhist sect.

Mandarin ducks, *oshi-dori,* being monogamous and remaining together for life, are symbolic of connubial affection. If separated they cannot be consoled and grieve themselves to death. They are featured with aquatic plants.

The butterfly, peony and cat combination is a popular theme in painting. The butterfly, *chocho,* is often found in paintings with the peony, morning-glory and chrysanthemum. Because of its metamorphosis from a caterpillar the butterfly symbolizes the immortal soul. A poem concerning a cat jumping from a peony bush after a butterfly immortalized the butterfly, peony, cat trio.

The heron, *shira sagi,* a symbol of purity, is frequently associated with the lotus flower because they both rise from muddy waters pure and unsullied. The heron is called The Thinker because of the way he stands on one leg with the other tucked under its wing, its head withdrawn and its eyes closed. *Yo* and *In,* light and dark, are represented sometimes by combining the white heron and black crow, *karasu.* The crow is a symbol of filial devotion because when the young are able to fly they show gratitude to their mother by feeding her for several weeks.

Especially beautiful attributes are given to trees, plants and flowers. Prominent in all the arts are three luck symbols *sho-chiku-bai* or pine-bamboo-plum. These are used always at New Year as well as at other times. The trio is also known as the Three Deities and Three Friends of Winter. Pine is a symbol of devotion because it is evergreen and its needles are usually in pairs representing conjugal love. It is also a symbol of longevity. Bamboo stands for strength and devotion. Though it bends with storms and snows it rises again when they have passed. The bamboo becomes stronger with age and is therefore an emblem of a long, healthy life. Plum, a harbinger of spring, represents chastity and virtue of womanhood as the cherry does of manhood because undaunted by the cold of winter the plum sends forth blossoms while the snow is still on the ground.

The cherry blossom, *sakura,* derived its name from a legendary princess to whom Mount Fugi is dedicated, Komo-Hana-no-Sakuya-Hime. It represents the beauty and charm of the Japanese countryside and is seen often enough to be considered the national flower. It rivals the chrysanthemum in the hearts of the Japanese but does not play so great a part in flower arrangement. A single cherry blossom is insignificant in itself but as part of a tree is an important unit. Similarly, an individual Japanese counts himself as nothing except as part of the universal whole.

The chrysanthemum, *kiku,* is another symbol of longevity and when represented with sixteen petals is the emblem of the Imperial family called the *kiku-no-go-mon.* If anyone else uses it the number of petals must be more or less then sixteen. The Empress has a crest too, a very elegant one made of three leaves and three flowers of the paulownia tree, *kiri.*

The beautiful lotus, *hasu,* is emblematic of purity, wisdom and Buddhahood. You see it on the altars of Buddhist temples and also in designs for articles used in the Buddhist service. You seldom see the white lotus used for secular purposes. It is symbolic of death and since most funerals in Japan are conducted under Buddhist rites the flower of the white lotus is associated with sad occasions.

Practically everything in Japan has symbolism. Certain combinations of plants and flowers are considered appropriate for specific occasions and festivals, and there are numerous rules and restrictions regarding their use. For instance cherry blossoms are never used in combination with anything except pine and must have the place of honor in the room; no other flowers may be displayed in its presence. But flower arrangements of pine and chrysanthemums can be used any time of the year for almost any occasion. It would be ridiculous for us to try to learn and observe all the Oriental symbols in our own arrangements but it is fascinating to learn all we can about them and it gives more depth to our own artistic expressions.

It has been said that

> "Obvious beauties are pleasing,
> Suggested beauties are delightful.
> Heard melodies are sweet
> But unheard melodies are sweeter."

THE JAPANESE FLORAL CALENDAR

In most countries flowers have a certain symbolic meaning, but nowhere are they so significant as in Japan. For centuries the flower of the month has been used in flower arrangement and has been a source of inspiration in all arts.

JANUARY pine *matsu*

The pine symbolizes long life because it always remains green and is a particularly strong and enduring tree. Some trees are over eight hundred years old possibly due to the fact that they are so well cared for. Pruning plays a great part in this and much time is spent in training the branches. The use of pine in floral art is considered a very good omen and thus it is an important element in floral compositions on all congratulatory occasions.

FEBRUARY   plum   *ume*

Plum stands for the beauty and virtue of women who are taught to be as noble as the *ume* flowers. They are highly valued for their fragrance and because they bring the dreariness of winter to an end with their beauty. Plum trees are much used in Japanese gardens. The branches of old ones are rugged, twisted, and moss-covered which makes them lovely to look at and to use in floral arrangements. These trees are not the kind commonly known in the West and although they bear fruit it is not eaten. The plum blossom because of its durability, sweet scent, classical simplicity, and beauty of form is much favored in floral compositions.

MARCH   peach   *momo*

Peach blossoms symbolize happiness in marriage and are loved and admired as very soft, delicate, and peaceful flowers signifying feminine virtues. The blossoms are always used during the girls' festival as decoration on the stands which hold the ceremonial dolls. The festival falls on the third day of March. Many weddings take place during this month when the peach blossoms are an attractive feature of the landscape.

APRIL   cherry   *sakura*

The cherry blossom symbolizes perfection and is worshipped and glorified as no other flower in Japan. Through the centuries it has been the theme of many poems. Cherry blossom time is a happy time and the whole nation celebrates. This tradition goes back to the ninth century. The blossoms are never used in flower arrangements for happy occasions because they die quickly and symbolize sudden death. The trees are not fruit bearing. The flowers, however, are sometimes used in brewing tea. Cherry is never used in combination with other plant material and has the place of honor in the *tokonoma* because it is the national flower of Japan.

MAY   peony   *botan*

The peony stands for prosperity because it retains its beauty so long and can be used to advantage in many kinds of arrangements. It is greatly loved in China where this plant originated. Traditionally it is one of the three flowers to which royal rank has been attributed, the other two being cherry blossom and lotus.

JUNE   iris   *shobu*

The iris stands for purity, innocence, and chastity. It is particularly used in arrangements during the boys' festival which falls on the fifth of May. The narrow swordlike leaves bring to mind things straightforward and upright. Many varieties are cultivated in Japan, and an iris garden is a magnificent sight. The iris flower is used in many kinds of arrangements.

JULY morning-glory *asagao*

The morning-glory symbolizes affection. The Japanese are perhaps the only people in the world who so enthusiastically arrange this flower. Large and beautiful varieties of many colors have been developed. Due to its prolific growth it has become known as "the poor man's flower." The morning-glory is used for hanging arrangements and usually alone.

A story treasured by the Japanese concerns Seno-Rikyu and a morning-glory arrangement. The great General Taiko Hideyoshi requested to see Rikyu's famed morning-glories and was invited to a morning tea ceremony. When he arrived at the famous tea master's home there was no sign of the flower. The ground was strewn with only sand and pebbles, but upon entering the tea room he encountered a sight of rare beauty. In the *tokonoma* was arranged a single morning-glory. Rikyu had destroyed his entire garden except for one perfect flower, thus emphasizing all the more the grace and beauty of the morning-glory.

AUGUST lotus *hasu*

The lotus, a water plant blooming in midsummer, symbolizes sincerity and nobleness and the flowers are closely associated with Buddhism. In a traditional lotus arrangement phases of existence: past, present, and future, are expressed by using seed pods, open leaves and flower, furled leaves and buds. It is a custom to form "early rising parties" to view these blossoms that open before dawn and close when the sun rises.

SEPTEMBER seven grasses of autumn *Akino nanakusa*

These grasses symbolize the coming of autumn and give seasonal color to any form of arrangement. They appear together in many Japanese paintings and have inspired many famous poets. The grasses are bush clover, *hagi;* pampas, *susuki;* kudzu vine, *kuzu;* pink, *nadeshiko;* patrinia, *ominaeshi;* thoroughwort, *fuji-bakama;* and Chinese bellflower, *kikyo.*

OCTOBER chrysanthemum *kiku*

The chrysanthemum, principal flower of fall, stands for immortality. Since the twelfth century it has been the emblem of the Imperial Court symbolizing peace, nobleness, and long life. This plant was introduced from China during the eighth century and through cultivation there are now more than five thousand varieties to demonstrate Japanese horticultural skill. The chrysanthemum is admired and honored and there are chrysanthemum viewing parties, a tradition that dates back centuries. Since the chrysanthemum flower lasts longer than most flowers it has come to be associated with longevity.

NOVEMBER   maple   *momiji*

The maple trees are at their best in November and their symbolic meaning is "faithful to the end." The branches are used in many kinds of flower arrangements, and a single branch combined with chrysanthemums typifies autumnal scenery.

DECEMBER   camellia   *tsubaki*

The camellia is the emblem of contentment and domesticity. Although it is admired for its exquisite beauty, it is sometimes avoided for festive occasions because of the way its flowers fall suggesting to the Japanese mind sudden death or a fall in prestige. Skill is necessary in making camellia arrangements because care is needed in trimming the leaves so that the flowers stand out to best advantage.

JAPANESE GARDENS AND HOUSES

III

The Japanese concept of a garden differs from that of other countries of the world which we have visited. Japan's strong national love of nature's beauty is an inherited and educated taste acquired through many centuries. The art of landscape gardening is one of their most articulate expressions of this great love. Their aim is to create a landscape picture of their countryside.

Japan is a beautiful country. In spite of its large population over half the land is covered with forest. In this mountainous island country most people live on the lowlands along the coast. The rocky, forested mountains rise behind them dominating the landscape. The sea is at their doorstep. Swift streams and rivers cascade down the mountain slopes to the sea leaving hillside pools and small lakes. This is the nature the Japanese know and love and interpret in their miraculous tiny gardens. The landscape designer carefully selects and modifies parts of a scene rather than producing a complete and realistic reproduction of nature. He captures the essence of reality and translates it to the garden much as an artist paints a landscape.

The gardens not only represent scenes of nature but express the philosophy, temperament, character and culture of the Japanese people. The proportions of these exquisite small gardens are so cleverly worked out that one forgets how tiny they are. They never seem crowded, and impart a sense of tranquility and idyllic calm.

As in the study of other gardens we can consider the art of Japanese gardens in relation to the judicious use of proportion, balance, color, unity of design, suitability, third dimensional values and on and on but there is no formula for one of the great ingredients—the spirit. There are many ways of presenting the same aspect of nature but usually the more literal they become the less they

51

contain of great art. Art is not a thing apart in Japan. Nature, life, and art flow into one another without a break. Art is not in a realm apart from and above nature and life. It is the perfection of them. The culture of the Far East is founded on intuitive vision.

The appreciation of beauty in nature is universal but the symbolic beauty the Japanese find in nature is unique. To the Japanese mind a garden is not only a place to cultivate trees and plants but a spot that provides simple relaxed and sentimental pleasure, seclusion, leisure, rest and meditation. One must realize this to fully appreciate the true significance of Japanese gardens. The deeper our knowledge of the Japanese art of landscape gardening, the greater will be our enjoyment when inspecting any garden.

The fundamental thing about Japanese gardens and flower arrangements that sets them apart from any other of the world is the fact that they are arts used to express the highest truths of religion and philosophy. This has been true in both China and Japan where these arts were used precisely as other civilizations have used the arts of literature and painting and ritual dance and music.

It is not necessary to become a disciple of Zen to use and enjoy Japanese gardening principles. Most Westerners do not desire to delve deeply into the subject. However, some understanding will heighten your understanding and appreciation of Japanese gardens.

The Western gardener can bring the calm, serene atmosphere and beauty of a Japanese garden into his surroundings by the careful placing of a few garden facilities and planting some trees and shrubbery. A fully Japanese garden which will blend perfectly with most Western-type houses is possible with a little extra contriving and study.

JAPANESE GARDEN ACCESSORIES

Japanese garden accessories with their romantic and historic connections contribute to the aesthetic value of the completed landscape picture. A garden can be just plants, shrubs, or trees or just lawn or sometimes just stones but if it is to be a success you must stress some part of it or call attention to some special feature. It must have one or more points of accent on which the strength of the unified whole can balance. These are especially important in a small garden. Although plants and trees can serve as points of focus it is perhaps easier and more effective to depend on objects such as stone lanterns, basins, pagodas, bridges, rustic resting places, stones or statuary. Proper accenting brings spaciousness and coherence to the garden. Decide first what you want to accent and then center your garden around these points from the very beginning. This will simplify the whole process of making a garden and avoid costly mistakes. Great care should go into the selection of garden features and they should be placed through the design of the garden in such a way as to appear as natural as the landscape itself.

Japanese Lantern, *Toro*

The most popular Japanese accessory used in Western gardens is the stone lantern (*ishi-toro*), which adds a touch of elegance to the garden scene. The stone lanterns are of pure Japanese origin and were used in Shinto shrines and Buddhist temples as votive lights and along the approaches to the shrines and temples for illumination. They came to be used in the garden for ornament and for lighting garden paths and the water basin. Through many centuries of use and refinement of garden lanterns there has naturally developed great variety in forms and sizes. The different styles have been named for temples or shrines, places of origin, or the people who designed them.

16. *A stone lantern—favorite Japanese accessory for Western gardeners—with two complementary stones.*

The usual height of a stone lantern is from five to six feet; however, since lanterns were originally used for practical purposes, some (such as those used to light a footpath) are from one to three feet high.

Of the many styles, one of the most frequently seen is the *kasuga,* which has a long cylindrical standard with a hexagonal lamp chamber and base, and a rounded hexagonal roof tilted at the eaves and topped by a flame-shaped finial. The sides of the hexagonal lamp chamber are open to allow for the insertion of an oil lamp or candle. The stone surfaces of the remaining four sides are carved with a buck, a doe, the sun, and the moon. The deer is the divine messenger of the Shinto Kasuga shrine at Nara. There are several other lanterns of similar form but with different names. Three thousand stone lanterns of many shapes line the approach to the Kasuga Shrine. These, along with a large number of hanging metal lanterns around the shrine buildings, are lighted two nights each year, once in February and again in August. I have been told that the shrine presents an unforgettable fairyland atmosphere on these two occasions.

Among the most charming of the small lanterns are the *yukimi-doro,* or snow-viewing lanterns, so called because the broad surface of the roof is designed to hold the snow in an outstandingly picturesque manner. These are usually from two to three feet tall and have no bottom pedestal but stands on widely spread legs. If set by the side of a pool or in the pool so that the water or bank is visible through the legs the lantern gives a dramatic bold effect. Although often the *yukimi* lantern is set on a flat stone or base, this is not a good practice as the pedestal conceals the clean lines of the design.

In Japan lanterns are almost never wired for electricity but are lighted with oil lamps or candles which produce a calm and serene atmosphere. The larger apertures of the light-housing section are fitted with panels of wood and translucent paper to further subdue the glow.

When choosing a lantern, size and proportion are of great importance as they must conform to the size and character of the garden. The modern trend is to use lanterns too large in scale for their surroundings and too many. Where more than one is used, each usually differs in size and design and setting. A lantern should be blended into the garden composition by proper placement of stones, shrubs or trees nearby. It is not generally effective to place a lantern in the middle of the lawn. They are better placed by a pool or water basin, along a path, or in some part of the garden where light is needed. If slightly masked by plants so they are partly hidden a feeling of depth will be achieved and the garden will have more feeling of quiet refinement. Usually a stone is placed one or two feet from the base of the lantern to give it a sense of stability and balance. It is better to turn the lantern so that the opening to the light compartment does not face the main point of view. Of course if you are lighting

17. (Left) A Kasuga-type stone lantern in an otherwise trite American garden scene.

18. (Right) This beautiful stone tower has eleven stories. Others have three, five, nine, and sometimes thirteen.

a pool, water basin, or the garden path have it face the area it is to light; nevertheless, do not forget that the important point is to give the garden a flavor of intimacy and mystery to suit your own personality and moods. If the lantern is carved the moon usually faces west and the star east but here again let the beauty and personality of the garden have first consideration.

Iron and bronze lanterns are also used. These are usually placed near the house and hung from the eaves or set on a rock.

Lanterns are not only admired for their beauty of form and the elegance they contribute to a garden but also for their age. Often special emphasis is placed on this and various methods are used to produce the appearance of age such as inducing lichen or moss to grow. Rubbing stone with buttermilk and keeping it in the shade to induce fungi to grow will give the appearance of age. A mixture of peanut butter and water rubbed on shaded stone will cause a brownish fungi to grow which produces a rust color on the stone.

Pagoda

A stone pagoda standing partially masked by trees or shrubs can, when properly placed, contribute much to the picturesque appearance of a garden. Tall ones of nine, eleven or thirteen tiers are suitable for a large hillside garden. Lower ones of three, five or seven tiers are attractive for smaller areas and by the side of a pool or lake where the reflection in the water is enchanting. Five tiered pagodas are the most popular in Japan. Five is considered auspicious because it represents the five directions, that is, the conventional four plus the center. Also five stories symbolize the five elements, earth, wood, fire, metal and water.

Pagodas are used as one of the most distinctive structures of a Buddhist temple compound. Originally they were only used as memorial or relic towers but today they generally serve no practical purpose and are largely ornamental and symbolic, symbolizing the supremacy of Buddha and the Buddhist law which towers above the earth and its people. Its function can be compared to that of the spire of the Christian Church. Although garden pagodas are usually of stone, temple ones are made chiefly of wood but may be of clay, tiles or bronze.

There are many types of garden pagodas which have no religious significance. Since their sole objective is to beautify the garden they represent only a fine piece of a stonecutter's art. Perhaps the loveliest style is the treasure tower which has compartments for lights. If there are three compartments there should be three lights and if there are five there should be five lights. These are indescribably beautiful at night when reflected in a pool of water.

In setting a pagoda in a Western garden one need not be concerned with symbolic carvings. The way you face it will depend on the garden, but generally speaking do not face it straight forward. It will be more effective and a sense of dimension will be achieved if you turn it slightly so that two sides show at once.

Basins

From ancient times water has been regarded as sacred in the Japanese garden. There are stations in some gardens where pure water is used to signify the washing away of uncleanliness from the soul as, for instance, in the tea garden where the concept is to purify the soul before entering the tea room.

Water basins can take many forms and sizes depending upon the taste of the individual. They are made in a variety of materials including stone, wood and pottery. They are used primarily for rinsing the hands and are often placed at strategic points along a garden path, outside a toilet or next to a veranda where it can be conveniently reached with a ladle while standing on the porch. These usually have appropriate low plantings of fern, severely clipped camellia, or various other low plants around the base. They often are backed up and partly surrounded by plantings.

19. *A beautiful example of one of the many types of water basins.*

In a *roji* garden of a tea house one of the first things one notices is the stone washbasin, *tsukubai,* with an intricate grouping of rocks. There is generally a large flat front stone, *mae-ishi,* on which to stand while using the basin. A stone called a *teshoku-ishi* on which to rest a candlestick or whatever one might be holding in one's hand is placed to the left of the basin. Another stone called *yuoke-ishi* on which to place a pail or pitcher is located to the right. Whenever a tea ceremony is held in winter a pail of hot water is provided on the *yuoke-ishi.* A lighted candle is provided on the *teshoku-ishi* for an evening or very early morning tea ceremony. A drainage basin, or *sea,* covered with gravel or pebbles is built under a *tsukubai* to take care of the discarded water and any overflow.

The water for a stone basin is usually furnished by one of two ways. It may be carried in each day in a pail and replenished or it may be filled and kept fresh by water dripping into it from a bamboo spout, *kakehi*. The spout is connected to a hidden pipe which is controlled from the house or by a faucet set in the ground near the basin and covered with a rock. A dipper is always provided at a water basin. These are generally made of cryptomeria or cypress wood. A Japanese water basin makes a lovely bird bath in a Western-type garden.

Garden Sculpture

In Japanese religion there are a host of Buddhas and Bodhisattvas and other subjects with significant symbolism. Sculptured deities are often used to give a strong spiritual quality to the garden. There is also an assemblage of household divinities called *shichifukujin* or seven gods of good luck. They occupy a prominent position in popular worship and are portrayed in a pleasantly humorous way, being endowed with human failings and an endless capacity for enjoyment. Hotei is probably the most popular of household deities. He is a lover of children and symbol of a happy life, portrayed as fat with a generous portion of his prominent belly showing, joyously laughing. In one hand he usually holds a fan while slung over his shoulder is a large bag in which he stows the Precious Things, *Takaramono*. A very large Hotei graces the lovely Japanese garden in Miami, Florida.

Crane and Tortoise

Figures of the crane and tortoise are often used as decorative accessories in Japanese gardens. Since these creatures are said to live longer than others, viewing a garden containing a crane and tortoise insures happiness and longevity.

Bridges

Of particular importance are the many kinds of garden bridges used for the purpose of getting people (or the eye of the viewer) across bodies of water, real or simulated. A Japanese bridge may be constructed of stone, wood, or earth and logs in a variety of styles ranging from the very simple and rustic to exceedingly elaborate ones. The design, size and material depends on the type of water barrier it is to span and the garden style. There is not a single garden bridge need in our Western gardens that some form of Japanese bridge cannot be found to fit superlatively.

20. (*Opposite, above*) *A graceful drum bridge spans a small stream.*

21. (*Opposite, below*) *A natural-rock bridge with unobtrusive anchor rocks in the ancient garden of Chishaku-in Temple, Kyoto, includes clipped evergreen azalea and box, with moss and some deciduous plants.*

My favorite bridges are the ones made of long wide planks laid zigzag fashion on wooden pilings and the rough stone-slab bridges. However, the elegantly arched cut-stone ones are beautiful. Some of these consist of several spans and are adorned with beautifully carved rail-posts. The arched wooden bridges are lovely but perhaps the most interesting bridges of all are the earth ones called *do-bashi*. These are made of bundles of small logs laid crosswise on a framework of timber. This is covered with about six inches of dirt and gravel and the sides of the bridge are then planted with turf which is secured with bamboo bound with cord to hold the soil in place.

Most Japanese bridges have a stone, post, or plants marking the edges to give a sense of safety. These warning devices are used in such a subtle and natural way that your steps are guided without your being aware of it. Bridges should be set when possible so that the sides are seen at an angle when viewed from the main point of regard.

Stepping Stones

Since the level portions of Japanese gardens are usually covered with sand or gravel or in many cases a well-swept hard surface of earth, a pathway is frequently made of *tobi-ishi*, skipping stones. There are numerous ways of laying stepping stones depending on the landscape and the esthetic senses of the designer, but the important thing to remember is that a relaxed and interestingly varied stride must be provided for in placing them. The height of the stones above the ground is one and one-half to two inches. In a tea garden they are two to three inches above the surface of the ground. Their tops should be reasonably flat and seven-eighths of the bulk of each stone buried to provide a stable walking surface.

The purpose of stepping stones in a Japanese garden is not simply the practical one for walking. Rikyu declared that stepping stones in a *roji* garden should be laid sixty percent for practicality and forty percent for looks. Later landscape designers advocated the reverse be practiced—sixty percent appearance and forty percent for practcal purposes. In any event, because *roji* means dewy path, a winding walk across woods or field with dewy vegetation alongside is kept in mind when laying stepping stones.

Unfortunately the best *roji* gardens with their beautiful stepping stones are missed on a guided tour of Japanese gardens because they are small and not generally publicized. Elegant simplicity, *kotan,* is the keynote of *roji.* Sometimes *roji* are planted with only a tree and a stone. In others *kotan* is achieved by planting one kind of plant such as bamboo or flowering cherry along the path. The *roji* covered with moss is beautiful but may be difficult to maintain. A sand paved *roji* is easy to keep up.

22. (Left) *The placement of stepping stones, seemingly casual, is planned in every detail.*

23. (Right) *An entrance walk of granite curbing and river rocks bordered by low hedges. If cement is required in a good Japanese garden—to hold small stones in a path or to line a pond or stream—it is kept below the surface or hidden by stonework or plantings.*

It may seem that I have digressed in discussing *roji* gardens under the heading of stepping stones but to the Western eye a *roji* may appear as a narrow path of stepping stones. In actuality that is all it is—a narrow path among a few trees or evergreens leading to the tea house. There are many situations in our landscaping where this type of garden could be charmingly adapted. Consider a *roji* as a connecting link between garden areas or perhaps it could solve the problem of a difficult narrow strip between two buildings.

Enclosures: Walls, Fences and Hedges

A Japanese thinks of his garden and house as one indivisible unit and separates it from the outside world by a variety of styles of walls, fences and hedges. The typical Japanese wall surrounding the older properties is of great thickness, constructed of clay in a framework of heavy timbers surmounted by a slanted roof of ornamental tile. These enclosures may also be made of stone, wood, bamboo or living plant material and combinations of these. The enclosures of the garden proper usually consist of fences not only for the whole garden but also in short

24. *The garden of Tenryuji Temple, Kyoto, illustrates the use of raked sand or gravel as ground cover. Here it is in dramatic contrast to a pool planted with water lilies. The garden "borrows" the scenery of Kameyama Hill and Mt. Arashiyama in the background.*

lengths as screens to divide a part of the garden or to hide something unsightly. Garden fences are considered ornamental pieces and the many kinds are unique and most interesting. They are made of many materials such as bamboo, wooden boards, plaited bamboo, reeds, rushes, and twigs. These materials are not only used alone but in a great variety of combinations and designs. These contribute a great deal of interest to the picturesque achitectural arrangement of the house and the garden. The most popular material for fence gates is bamboo or a combination of bamboo and reeds and rushes. Some very interesting sleeve-fences, *sode-gaki*, are made from these materials too. They consist of a single unit of gatelike form three or four feet wide and from five to seven feet high and are used to conceal something but are actually very ornamental.

Garden walls, fences, hedges and shrubs and tree screens are never made high enough to completely cut off the outside world. Since land is scarce and most gardens are small the garden builder tries to gain whatever expansion of view that is possible without sacrificing privacy. He plans his garden to take advantage of the view of a distant mountainside or his neighbor's pine or a bamboo grove. This is called *shakkei*, borrowed scenery.

62

Water

From ancient times water has been regarded as sacred in gardens in both the East and the West. This is especially true in Japanese gardens where pure water may be brought and poured into the water basin to wash away uncleanliness from the soul. The Japanese love all aspects of water—still, running, dripping and falling. It is most highly esteemed when it moves or makes a noise. When it is not feasible to make a stream or pond in a garden the presence of water is suggested. Sometimes a dry stream bed is laid out with plants and rocks arranged along the edges of the sandy course. Or a level area of white gravel is raked into wave patterns to suggest an ocean shoreline. Rocks are used to symbolize islands in the expanse of sand-covered ground.

Japan being an island country surrounded by ocean, a land of abundant rainfall filling streams, lakes, and rice paddies, it is no wonder that its gardens have contained water features (both real and simulated) since ancient times. A murmuring stream winding through a garden injects a feeling of movement in an otherwise passive scene. Waterfalls, ponds, lakes, and islands are all important features of the Japanese garden scene.

25. The Japanese garden designer achieves some of his most charming effects by the way in which he guides one's footsteps across water. Stepping stones at lower left contribute a sense of adventure to a stroll through the garden.

Sand Designs

An expanse of sand in the garden gives a feeling of infinite extensibility. Wide open spaces of white sand are not accidental but are left vacant to stimulate the imagination and induce the creating of the viewer's own ideas—not just an echo of the artist's dream. It is said that true beauty can be discovered only by those who mentally complete the incomplete. When imagination is unconfined it constructs its own rich scenes. The aim of Zen is to calm and concentrate the mind so it can be spiritually awakened. It is not surprising that Zen devotees turn to the garden which is a composition in space in their meditation and search for *satori*. Therefore, the dominating feature in these gardens was stone

26. *At Daisen-in Temple in Kyoto gray pebbles are raked in a pattern symbolizing the sea of nothingness. The meaning of the two piles of sand may be sought in the mind of the beholder—pilgrims, children and sightseers deep in contemplation or young Zen priests tending the garden who are often found seated in disciplined meditation. The garden is enclosed by a double hedge of privet which links the trees outside and the sand garden. In one corner a sakaki tree, sacred in Buddhist religion, softens the severity of the straight lines and relates the garden to the natural landscape outside.*

arrangements and to these were added sand, moss, and neatly trimmed low trees or shrubs leaving uncluttered space. Thus the interpretation of the resulting composition is left to the person who comes to appreciate and to meditate.

The rock and sand gardens of Japan are simple abstractions of nature. They are usually made in small, flat spaces enclosed by fences, hedges or walls. The "sand" used is usually white or light grey crushed stone of the size a Western gardener would call fine gravel. This is laid two or three inches thick over hard-tamped earth. The designs raked into the sand by a bamboo rake generally symbolize aspects of still or flowing water. They may be simple parallel lines, straight or wavy undulations symbolizing water in a stream or eddying into a shoreline. The sand sometimes is raked into complicated designs such as a series of concentric circles representing raindrops falling into a pool making ever-widening circles.

Sound

The Japanese gardener does not overlook sounds in the garden. A grove of bamboo or pine is often planted so the trees catch the wind. The sound of rain being wind-driven through a grove of bamboo trees is a memorable experience. We are all familiar with the haunting sounds of oriental wind chimes.

The sound of water dripping from a bamboo spout into a pool or stone basin, the splash of water falling from a cascade, and the babbling brook rushing over rocks are all pleasant to the ear.

Singing insects are dear to the hearts of the Japanese people. The insect season begins on May 28 and at that time the insect seller appears with his wares. He need not advertise his stock in trade as the chirping crickets and other singing insects in their small cages attract the buyers who hang the cages on trees under the eaves of their houses where during the hot summer nights the garden stillness is broken by the songs of the insects. In late August or September the insect-hearing festival is a picturesque rite. Old and young gather in various gardens carrying their insects in tiny cages, some of which have been brought from their own gardens and others that have been bought from vendors especially for the ceremony of "Freeing the Insects." The cages are opened and the tiny captives freed. Then almost breathless the liberators wait for the insects to get their bearings, realize they are free, and send forth their rejoicing songs.

TYPES OF JAPANESE GARDENS

Japanese gardens have been classified into three classes: hill, flat, and tea garden.

Tea Garden, *Cha-niwa*
Described in Chapter 2 under Tea Ceremony.

Hill Garden, *Tsukiyama-niwa*

This is the most complete landscape garden and as the name implies contains a hill, a group of hills or a range of hills representing a mountain ridge. Often there are five principal hills which represent actual mountain scenery with a distant peak, the sweeping contours of nearer mountains and low rounded hills in the foreground. The remote mountains have little detail because they represent mountains at great distance and are veiled in mystery. The near mountains have a fair amount of detail in the form of rocks and plants. Sometimes the view of distant mountains outside the garden can be "borrowed" and used as part of the over-all design.

Of great importance in this type of garden is the principle of suggesting to the imagination the impression of space by the use of blank spaces and obliterations.

The elevations are usually combined with a water feature such as a pond or stream. Looking at the garden from the house the hills are usually in the background and the pond and stream in the foreground. Often the pond has at least one rocky island on it planted with grass, low shrubs, and one or more picturesquely bent pine.

27. The Golden Pavilion, Kinkakuji, has historic and aesthetic interest for everyone interested in Japanese plant crafts. The garden contains a beautiful pond with many large and small islands. It nestles harmoniously at the foot of Mt. Kinugasa and there is no break in the planting from the pond's edge to the top of the mountain.

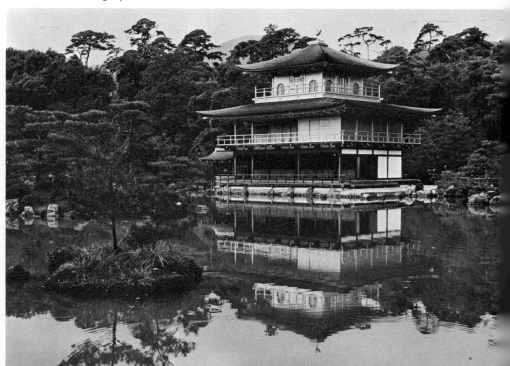

The idea of islands originated in Chinese lore and bear descriptive names. There are four important ones according to the rules for gardens. The first is *horaijima,* island of the blessed, which is supposed to be an island in the sea and is placed in the center of the lake. Six rocks grouped around it symbolize a tortoise with stones representing the head, legs, and tail. A picturesque pine tree is usually placed in the center because both the tortoise and the pine are symbolic of longevity.

The second island is called *fukiagejima,* wind-swept isle, and being a sea island is not connected with a bridge.

The other two islands are called *shujinto,* master's isle, and *kiakujinto,* guest's isle. The master's isle is placed in the foreground and sometimes has a small shelter or summer house on it and can be reached by a bridge. The guest's island is placed in the background of the landscape and is also approached by a bridge and stepping stones.

A Japanese garden is skillfully arranged to compensate for limited area by hiding parts of the contour with plants and shrubbery. Thus by careful planning the conception of a large lake is suggested to the imagination because it is never completely visible from any point. The suggestion of limitless space by partial deletion of contour lines used in Japanese paintings is used equally in the art of landscape gardening.

A hill garden is not complete without a real or suggested waterfall or cascade. According to the principles of garden design a tree should be placed so that its branches conceal the outlet of the cascade and foliage should surround it to give an appearance of depth and remoteness.

A path winds through the garden which allows the spectator to stroll along pausing at those spots that afford the most beautiful or picturesque views. The garden is planted with pines and other evergreen shrubs and trees which give it an appearance of being alive and flourishing throughout the year. They are combined with an occasional planting of deciduous trees and shrubs providing blossoms or colorful foliage at different seasons. Ground covers may be moss, low bamboo, low trimmed shrubs such as azalea or yew, lawn grass or gravely sand. These may be used alone or in combination.

Water basins are placed at appropriate points and stone lanterns are used at various places to furnish light for walking in the garden at night and for special events such as snow-viewing parties.

Flat Garden, *Hira-niwa*

In contrast to the hill garden is the flat garden. This type is laid out on a level enclosed area and represents either a mountain valley or a seacoast scene

28. *The most celebrated of all Japanese gardens, the centuries-old temple garden of Ryoanji in Kyoto, is undoubtedly the finest example of the flat type. On a sea of sand fifteen stones are arranged in groups of five, three and two. The only planting is a bit of moss at the bases of the stone groupings. An exceptional tile-roofed plaster wall encloses the garden.*

with rocks sometimes arranged to suggest islands in the sea. Rock and shrubs clipped in rounded forms are often grouped to suggest mountain scenery. The flat portion is covered with white gravelly sand, lawn grass, moss, or a combination of these to represent the sea or the flowing water of a stream. This type of garden is called dry landscape, *kare-sansui*, and its charm lies in the effect its abstract symbolism produces in the mind of the beholder who interprets the scene according to his own imagination.

The Ryoanji garden in Kyoto is one of the finest examples of dry-landscape style. Its fifteen stones are grouped in five sets of two, three or five with perfect proportion on the level white gravelly sand raked in meticulously worked patterns. Such masterful use of space has never been expressed so eloquently and symbolically. To some the rocks suggest the legend of *tora-no-ko watashi* in which tigers led their cubs across a mountain stream. To others they represent an expanse of clouds or islands in the sea. It is an awe-inspiring thing to experience this garden in the daytime but I have been told that on a clear moonlit night the rocks appear as living things of nature.

Another famous dry landscape garden is Daisen-in, one of the smaller monasteries in the compound of Daitokuji temple in Kyoto. Like Ryoanji it is a miniature of nature confined to a small space. See illustration 11 and 12.

MAGIC OF STONES AND TREES

Stones play a very essential part in the Japanese garden and are the backbone of the total design. The Japanese consider them even more important than trees due perhaps to an Oriental aspiration for eternity and an attempt to add the eternal element that is found in nature to the garden. Rocks can arouse a sensation of power and aspiration or a feeling of tranquility. The Japanese feel life and soul in stone and believe that if it is imbued with understanding the inner spirit will spring to life.

They use two approaches to grouping rocks, a realistic duplication of nature and an aesthetic representation of it. To the perceptive Oriental mind rocks may suggest a precipice, mountain range, or chain of islands. Having used stones from ancient times they have developed a high degree of appreciation of natural rocks and consider a moss-covered stone the ultimate in beauty. The subtle refinement, or the *shibusa,* with which moss veils the beauty of stones is in great favor. The first line of the Japanese national anthem points this up by expressing the wish that His Majesty the Emperor's days may continue until the gravel has grown into boulders and is covered with moss.

For centuries beautiful stones from the mountains near Kyoto have been highly treasured. Especially fine stones were handed down generation after generation and often war lords appropriated particularly beautiful ones. A famous stone, the Fujito stone, at Sambo-in near Kyoto has belonged to at least four gardens. It is said to have been brought to its present location wrapped in fine silk and to the sound of music.

Fortunately almost every country of the world is filled with a great variety of fine metamorphic rock equal to that found in Japan.

29. *A Japanese garden in winter showing trees (cycas palm) protected from the cold with rice-straw coverings, whose natural texture and color add their own sculptural form. Note the graceful, slightly arched stone-slab bridge and the use of rocks along the "river" of raked sand.*

Every Japanese garden uses rocks in some form. Superlative stones are often placed in a position to be enjoyed purely for their ornamental value and are treated as the garden treasures they are rather than as points in the general design. Sometimes they have a specific function or decorative purpose such as water basin, lantern, bridge, steps or path. But often a stone is used in combination with other stones, plantings or sand to suggest a natural scene or to create an abstract design. Sometimes an interesting stone combined with a planting becomes the dominant design element in a grouping or major point of interest in the garden scene.

The variety of shapes of natural stones is limitless but they have been divided into five major categories called *gogyseki* or five natural stones. *Gogyo,* or the division of all things into five elements, is derived from ancient Chinese learning. The Japanese borrowed the characters representing these elements —wood, fire, earth, metal and water—and applied them to the five classes of stone—shapes as follows:

1. *Taido,* wood. Tall Vertical. Suggests high rising trees. Sometimes called body stones. Placed in rear of a grouping.

2. *Reisho,* metal. Low Vertical. Suggests the stability of metal. Frequently placed with tall verticals. Sometimes called soul stones.
3. *Shigyo,* fire. Arching. Branches energetically to sides as fire does. Called stone atmosphere and peeping stones. Usually placed to the front and slightly to one side of other shapes.
4. *Shintai,* water. Flat or Horizontal. Called mind and body stone or level base stones. Most frequently used harmonizer for rock groupings.
5. *Kikyaku,* earth. Reclining. Also known as root or prostrate stones. Placed in foreground to give final touch of harmony.

If Westerners will study the Japanese classification of stones and become familiar with their shapes and masses it will be a great help in working out agreeable combinations for our gardens.

30. *A print from an old scroll demonstrates the artistic placement of various shapes of stone.*

Arranging Rocks or Stones

The Japanese approach to placing rocks or stones is very different from the Western technique of making a rock garden. Great attention is paid to each rock's individual character, its relationship to plant materials to be used and to the architectural elements, and to the design of placement. The over-all design and the role of all the components (architecture, plant and rock) are carefully considered. In the actual placing of stones and plants the design is assembled by the same principles of heaven, man and earth placement as observed in flower arrangements. In all the arts the Japanese show their devotion to asymmetry in their use of triads, the quantity of three, the triangle. The imaginary triangle in a Japanese garden is never equilateral, therefore balance is occult rather than evident. Rocks and plants are banked up both laterally and in depth with each element masking portions of the element adjacent to it. They are never monotonous but are grouped sculpturally to act as strong lines and transitional elements. Rocks are never scattered haphazardly in a composition or set too prominently. The aim is to create a pleasing contrast of vertical and horizontal forms

31. (Left) Rocks give composure to plants by conveying a feeling of permanence and are the backbone of this garden. The rocks follow the same principles of heaven, man, and earth placement as observed in flower arrangement.

32. (Right) Every stone has been precisely placed and blended with plants to appear uncontrived.

with a feeling of subtle harmony. There are many possible combinations and by intelligently contrasting different masses and heights pleasing effects are not difficult to achieve.

According to the Law of Connection there should be an intimate relationship between rock, plant material and water. Rounded stones taken from a river bed are best used to mark the course of a garden stream. Rocks of rugged form found in the· mountains conform more naturally as symbolic mountains in a garden. One rock is rarely set alone but if it is of good size or appears as a natural outcropping it is permitted.

The Japanese gardener studies nature and in setting rock in a garden he almost intuitively knows which side to turn to view. He tries always to discover the "living face" to expose to view and buries much of the rock's bulk below the surface of the ground. When it is in position it looks as if it belongs there —that it is firmly rooted in the soil and has been there since the beginning of time.

Rocks give composure to plants by conveying a feeling of solidity and permanence. Plants complement rocks by softening the lines. An especially lovely effect and a feeling of quietness is achieved by setting a large flat rock or group of rocks by a perpendicular tree such as a pine. Rocks in thickets of oak, pine, cryptomeria, or other needle evergreen create the feeling of a forest. *Camellia japonica* and *Sasanqua* are particularly charming snuggling against a rock, but very large-leafed shrubs such as aucuba are not planted over rocks lest the rocks sour and "die."

Trees

Trees and shrubs are planted only after all the principal stones have been laid, and careful consideration is given these because the stones can serve their proper purpose only when this addition is correctly made.

According to the rules of Japanese gardening there are certain positions considered best for planting trees. The designer is careful to place trees and shrubs in situations to conform with their natural habitat. For instance a mountain tree is not planted in a valley, or vice versa. With the exception of the plum tree which blooms early in the year trees that shed their leaves are not planted in the foreground. The mouth of a cascade is one of the choice positions for a tree for here it will produce an effect of lonely remoteness. By a pool is another favorite place because of the shadows it casts on the water. Pine trees of bending formation are often placed at the edge of a lake with long branches trained to stretch out over the water. Frequently these are supported by props. A tree is always planted near the tea house to partly conceal it from view. Trees of various kinds are planted by wells and water basins for shade and for mirroring in the water of the basin.

33. *The garden of Sambo-in Temple, Kyoto, illustrates the magic of trees and stones. The garden consists also of a pond, waterfalls, bridges and islands. The total beauty is enhanced by "borrowing" the remote view of Mt. Daigo in the background.*

The names applied to trees in a Japanese garden will give a clue to other functions. The "principal" tree, usually a large, beautifully proportioned pine or oak, should occupy the most prominent position. Next in importance is the "view-perfecting" tree, and after that the "setting sun" tree, often a maple that turns red in autumn, is placed so the rays of the setting sun can be seen through it. There is a "distancing pine" and a tree of "solitude" which suggests a mood of meditation. A "light-interfering" tree is planted close to a stone lantern to hide part of it, and there is often a "overhanging-the-gate" tree.

Many flowering trees and shrubs are used along with those of brilliant foliage. Some popular ones are camellia, azalea, gardenia, cherry, plum, peach, wisteria, and fall-coloring maples.

The most loved and used tree in Japan is the pine. When you arrive, whether by air or by sea, you will be at once struck by the fact that pine trees

74

dominate the scenery of both the countryside and the gardens. In the garden this king among trees is given untiring attention to see that they retain their ideal appearance. The *matsu,* or native pine, is of rugged irregularity, but the Japanese gardener will skillfully group its needles into clumps having a somewhat flat and rounded form. To prevent the clumps of needles from becoming too large and full the gardener will pull out by hand all except perhaps a dozen needles in each clump.

In pruning and other landscape treatment of trees the exaggeration of the natural characteristic is practiced. In the nursery, the pine for the garden receives extensive surgery. Branches are bent or broken and bound with cord and splints to produce forms of unusual beauty. Such pine trees are often depicted in Japanese paintings and scrolls and in other decorative arts.

There is an old Japanese saying about the virile and enduring pine tree: *Fu ro sen nen no aki,* "It never fades even throughout a thousand autumns."

Bamboo in wide variety is used as a growing plant but more especially as a garden building material for fences, etc.

Trees and shrubs of one species are often grouped together in mass to get an effect of strength and substance. For example pine, bamboo, cryptomeria, cypress, oak or birch are often planted as a grove or thicket. However, sometimes for the purpose of contrast in form, color or texture, a deciduous tree such as a maple is planted among a group of evergreens. In planting three or more trees or in setting three or more rocks care is taken so that they are not in one line either in depth or breadth.

Broad-leafed deciduous trees should never be planted over needle-bearing evergreens. It is better to plant them under the evergreens to allow some sunlight to filter through to the deciduous plants beneath.

Japanese Pruning

Most Western landscape architects will tell us how and where to plant trees and shrubs but never how to keep them growing within bounds and full of life and vigor year after year and generation after generation. This is an area where the Japanese art of pruning trees and shrubs, which is highly developed, can be of inestimable value to the gardener both through contributing to the lasting beauty of the garden and the practical aspect of not having to replace overgrown plants after a few years. In the gardens and parks of Japan, trees and shrubs are trimmed and kept at the same size and shape for centuries. Their method of pruning not only regulates size but stimulates and rejuvenates. They think nothing of moving an eighty-year-old pine tree with relatively no root pruning and very little removal of foliage. A tree that has been trimmed for

34. *Trees and large shrubs can be kept small and healthy for generations through proper pruning. Camellias in Japan grow into large trees but in this garden of a Japanese inn they have been kept low and trailing for years. Their waxy leaves provide exquisite textural contrast to the coarseness of large stones.*

many years comes to possess the virtue of showing no damage or checking of vitality as a result of transplanting.

There is no magic about the techniques of training and controlling the shape of trees and shrubs as practiced by Japanese gardeners for generations. They are in truth simple and practical. The gardener in the West can accomplish the same effect. First decide on the artistic effect desired then using imagination and common sense proceed and see the dynamic changes that take place as the tree gets older. If you feel that a particular straight branch is without interest, cut it off above a bud or another branch. The remaining lower portion will then become the main branch and receive the nourishment that formerly went to the part you removed. Now instead of growing straight out the limb will turn or curve.

Another good pruning practice for artistic appearance is to cut out straight side branches that ascend upward and do not parallel other more horizontal branches. These almost vertical branches are in reality suckers of several years' growth which were not cut out when they first appeared.

The training of branches on horizontal bamboo poles so that they grow into an arrangement of lines and ridges is another favorite method that has been practiced since ancient times and is carried to perfection in many of the Zen monastery gardens.

Shrubs are often pruned into rounded or hemispherical forms to represent mountain scenery. The juniper varieties, sasanquas and camellias are favored for this type of pruning.

Besides aesthetic reasons and the desire to control excessive growth and spread, plants are pruned and trimmed for horticultural purposes. Pruning may occasionally be done to rejuvenate a plant by cutting it down to the stump which stimulates the growth of healthy new shoots. This is practiced on privets, laurels, willows, birches, rhododendrons and sometimes camellias. Cutting out suckers and parallel branches also serves to rejuvenate a plant. Dead or diseased wood should of course be removed from a tree or shrub at any time it appears.

The pruning, trimming, and other treatments practiced on trees exaggerate some of the natural characteristic forms, but at the same time keep the form in the closest harmony with nature.

The techniques used when working with the dominant tree of Japan, the black pine, are applicable to other kinds of evergreen and deciduous trees. The best times to prune a pine are May and September but it can be done anytime from September until June.

The Japanese consider a low spreading shape the most beautiful and expressive of the pine's personality. This characteristic shape with its long, low lateral branches extending far out from the trunk giving the feeling of wing-like floating is the result of yearly pruning, pinching and plucking started in early growth. Although each limb follows a generally straight course away from the trunk it is actually a series of twists and turns which keep the branches growing on a single course. This type of pruning allows the sunlight to penetrate down to even the lowest limb of the tree and it remains vigorous after many years of growth.

Removal of Buds and Needles

If terminal buds are left on the limbs they will stretch upward and out extending the dimensions of the tree. To control the spread of the branches the tip of the young tender bud at the end of each twig is pinched off leaving about an inch of the bud. Nearby latent buds will thus be stimulated to grow but the shoots they produce will be shorter and more crowded than those the removed bud would have produced. If this is done in April or May dense needles will sprout during the spring and summer. In September a second trimming is done. The needles which have sprouted below the bud along the previous year's growth are plucked off. This gives the tree a light and floating appearance and allows sunlight and rain to penetrate into the branches. Generally up to one half the number of needles produced are removed. It depends on where the shoot is located and its vigor. The higher and further out the position of the shoot, the more needles are removed. The removed pine needles are useful in the garden as ground cover or winter protection for small plants.

Cutting Back

From time to time cutting back will be necessary to shorten branches, to thin out branches, to open space for new growth, to equalize and balance, to rejuvenate certain branches or the whole tree and to make the branches lower and more widely spread on older trees.

Supports

Many of the lower branches of trees are supported by neat props. This keeps long branches from sagging as they age, permits the lower branches to extend to prevent a leggy appearance of the tree, prevents snow damage and is also a safety precaution for trimmers working on the branch and the branch itself.

Cloud Pruning

Many Japanese trees have the over-all appearance of layers of foliage laid irregularly over each other with space between each layer. This has the effect of clouds or layers of mist and is called *sashide*. The technique consists mainly of the cutting out of the main tip branches and pruning off the small branches which project downward thus achieving an upward sweeping tufty look. This not only produces a beautiful appearance but the cutting out of excess branches opens up the tree permitting the sun's rays to filter down to the foliage of the lower limbs.

A Japanese gardener will study the character of each tree and adjust his pruning methods accordingly. Just as each tree has its own peculiar habits and requirements, each landscape gardener has his own peculiarities and preferences. These differences in pruning methods are discernible even in gardeners trained under the same teacher. In Japan a keen observer can tell if a tree has been trimmed by the same gardener year after year. In other words whether one is looking at a work of creative art or the work of an outstanding craftsman distinctive taste, style, and skill are always discernible.

Planning the Garden

In planning a garden the Japanese landscape artist employs both aesthetic and physiological principles to achieve his effects. He has a profound understanding of nature's forms and also he knows how men respond to them physiologically, emotionally, and intellectually. He knows that such a simple thing as arranging the stepping stones can make a person walk either awkwardly or gracefully and feel pleasure or irritation. He tries not to show everything in the garden from one spot but tries to create mystery and stimulate the imagination. Each view withholds some part of itself—the garden path turns, disappearing behind rock or shrub. By making a path turn at a certain point the builder makes the spectator walking there turn and pause and direct his eye to a particularly interesting view. The purpose of the zigzag bridge is to cause one to slow down, pause and enjoy the scenery. It is as though the garden designer were always there leading you through the garden, pointing out what is beautiful to see and experience.

The close wedding of the garden scene and the home is achieved by spending many days contemplating the site in varied weather and at all hours of the day. The garden planner makes little use of plans and sketches but carries a basket of pegs which he occasionally drives in the ground as he walks. Here and there he sets up a high bamboo pole to which have been lashed crosspieces that represent the spread of the branches of some tree he plans to bring in. Thus he visualizes by degrees the whole area of the garden constantly returning to one or another part of the grounds to make sure the vista is preserved or that a distant path is revealed. The scene develops and changes under his hand. When the stream is finished its angles and its curves are those of nature. The beaches are in the coves where running water would deposit its load of sand. Much is mere copying of nature's way of working and in that sense it is just like the work of the landscape painter who contrives his own compositions. When all is finished imagine yourself sitting in an open room of the house drinking tea and looking out. You see water glint but what its farthest stretch is you do not know. The suggestion is that the stream flows on and on through pleasant country to the ocean far away. The stepping stones that cross its narrowest place lead the eye to a dip on the other side and then it appears again and once more hides in a thicket beyond. Thus you experience Zen practice in the teasing charm of incompleteness—the suggestion that the onlooker finish his own idea according to his own imagination.

JAPANESE GARDENS FOR AMERICANS

Today the tendency to combine Western-style living with Japanese gardens is growing. Some landscape architects are endeavoring to evolve a new type of garden based on the traditional Japanese appreciation of nature but designed in a way less dependent on the legends and mandatory rules of the old Japanese gardens. There is hope that this influence will help to lift the garden designs of the West from the monotonous rut in which we have been entrenched. Japanese design can inspire new attitudes and a fresh approach to designing and planting our gardens.

Stones are being used in a free way resulting in Ryoanji-type sand and stone gardens ancient in concept but quite contemporary in form. In city gardens where space is at a premium and areas are so surrounded by buildings that air and light are shut out combinations of sand, stones and controlled planting are becoming more and more popular. Gardeners are finding that Japanese gardens and gardening techniques can contribute immeasurably to contemporary living. This branch of landscape design lends itself admirably to today's need for conservation of space and low maintenance. I believe that the marriage of the Western- and Japanese-type gardens will eventually result in types of gardens differing from the traditional Japanese garden but closely governed by the same old universal laws of design which determine form and the enduring quality of a true artistic expression. The greatness of any garden lies in the

35.   *A corner of the tea garden in Watson Park in Miami, Florida, shows the* yoritsuki *(waiting room) and* roji *(dewy path). The lovely small stone lantern is just right for lighting a garden path at night.*

degree to which the laws of art have been employed in its design, the unifying and tempering of angles and textures that time must bring, and above all the presence of "spirit" in a garden which overcomes minor defects. The good Japanese garden ties man to nature and is not too concerned with the complex. Instead it expresses itself in simple things such as stones rooted to the earth by moss and plants, water perhaps not too fussily clean, trees grown or trained to aged forms, and most important of all complete exclusion of the mundane world.

No type of garden is perfect or universal in appeal nor is it always in tune with ever-changing human needs. There are gardens for all kinds of personalities. All reflect the designers' taste and the limitations of the time and place. Some Japanese gardens are greatly overdone and mixed in design, but don't dismiss any of them lightly as unworthy of study. As in all countries Japan has had its periods of greatness and its eras of bad taste. The introduction of Western ideas during the last hundred years has greatly disturbed and influenced gardening in Japan but in spite of outside influences gardens of all periods have shown wonderful sensitivity and understanding of the needs of the time. Always there has been an awareness of the relationship of the garden to the home, to living and to aspirations of the human heart.

Planting

The planting of a Japanese garden is based on the idea of creating a permanent picture composition of a true or imaginary landscape scene for all seasons. Just as a natural view is beautiful in summer or winter the man-made landscape must never be unattractive. Many simple but practical ideas are followed to obtain this result. These often are only common sense.

Evergreens make up the main mass of planting and are banked around the edges of the garden or arranged in clumps. Streams and ponds are edged or accented with massed evergreens. When deciduous trees or shrubs are used they are backed by evergreens to preserve the permanent scene. Cut flowers are grown elsewhere with the exception of lotus planted in lakes and iris at the edge of ponds and streams. Flowering shrubs are used more for year-round beauty than for their blooms. Plants such as camellias, azaleas, gardenias and daphne lend color and fragrance in season as well as year-round form to the garden. Moss, low ground covers, and berried shrubs offer contrast and add delicate notes. The king of trees, pine, and other dense evergreens serve as a canopy and frame for the over-all picture. A distinct gain we can acquire from a study of Japanese gardens is a naturalistic touch that our gardens sorely need.

The refined Japanese have always frowned upon making a garden an ornamental appendage to the house or making an ostentatious display. Their attitude is that gardens should be pleasant retreats for hours of leisure and meditation and should be made from a genuine love of nature. The landscape gardeners are said to have expressed various sentiments in their works such as long life and happiness, pleasure of retirement, gentleness and many others. Whether awe-inspiring, gay, placid or solitary these fanciful conceptions are inspired by the emotions aroused by natural scenery.

The famous old gardens were not designed by professional landscape designers but by Buddhist priests, tea masters, architects and artists. Through love of nature, refined taste, and a basic sense of design they have organized space with wondrous economy of material.

Maintenance

One of the chief advantages of a Japanese garden is that it can be kept neat in appearance and in good condition without much care. That is not to say no care because even an expanse of sand will become littered and require raking. A well-kept Japanese garden has an orderly and well-groomed appearance despite its naturalism and asymmetry. General cleanings are given in spring

36. *The well with two ancient battered buckets dominates this tiny garden. The only maintenance it requires is an occasional brushing and a bit of pruning once or twice a year.*

and fall when everything is given a very thorough going-over. All trees and shrubs are carefully pruned, clipped, sheared, pinched or plucked, and even the smaller branches of the large trees are thinned and new shoots pruned. The hidden artistic potential of each plant is discovered and the most interesting qualities are emphasized, eliminating distracting elements and simplifying the lines. Thus a tree ar shrub may become to a degree an abstraction. Even if the form is naturalistic it may also symbolize grander elements of the natural landscape.

Between these intensive general cleanings and groomings the average Japanese garden needs only a minimum of care. Since there are no flower beds and usually no lawns the upkeep is a joy and not drudgery. It amounts to lightly raking around shrubs; removing dead leaves, blossoms and weeds; sweeping; and keeping an eye open for diseases or insects.

The Japanese have learned that it is wrong to bury the house in an overabundant mass of plants so that it loses its own personality. The lines of the buildings are only complemented by the planting around it, never concealed. Each serves as a foil for the other and the house is closely joined to its garden environment in one balanced unified composition. The restrained and artful arrangement of trees, shrubs, moss, rocks and water features lead the architecture into the landscape. All of this suggests the partnership of nature and man and the transition is never abruptly made. It is a gradual, subtle and logical progress going in both directions and unifying the home and garden into an indivisible whole.

Making a Garden Appear Larger

We in America use broad sweeps of lawn to set off our gardens. These lawns are expensive to plant and to maintain. We can learn from the Japanese how to use less space but still create a feeling of space that is interesting and requires lower upkeep. The Japanese are experts at disguising the actual size of a garden and making a big event out of a small area. Soami, a famous sixteenth century tea master and designer of gardens, said:

"However small a garden may be it can be made to include high mountains many miles away, and to create waterfalls of tremendous height. There is a method of including distant waters and the vast expanse of the ocean. All this is possible by knowing how to handle water and rocks.

"The ultimate aim of the landscape garden is to reveal the mysteries of nature and creation. This may be achieved by a simple flat garden with only a few rocks. However interesting may be the pattern, and beautiful the scenes, the truth of the hills may be lost if the garden is lacking in coherence...

37. *Here is the very spirit of tranquility and timelessness. Easily and naturally the eye progresses from object to object. This composition in stone has great refinement and exemplifies the quality of* shibusa. *No garden could be easier to maintain.*

"Even in a limited area, a landscape suggestive of the heart of a mountain or a deep ravine can be created. Take for instance the case of a waterfall. If the waterfall is exposed to a full view from the top to the bottom, it will appear low and add very little to the scenic effect. But if the upper part is concealed by trees, the middle part partially hidden by a projecting rock or a branch of a tree, and the basin has a growth of grass or plants, then the fall may give the impression of a great height.

"It is the same with a pond. If it is large and square or has nothing to hide any part of it, one can see it all at a glance, and nothing is left to the imagination. Whereas the pond may be small, with winding contours partly concealed by trees and rocks, but may give the impression of a large lake or bay that might hint at an expanse of sea beyond.

"When a real tea master lays out a garden, he will try to conceal his art so that his work will look natural, and to create a deep forest or valley, even if a place may be surrounded by city dwelling houses."

The illusion of depth is accomplished by numerous changes of plant material and levels of planting. By the use of larger trees and shrubs and those with large leaves near the house and smaller trees of finer textured leaves farther away the illusion of greater distance is created. When trees and shrubs are grouped to form a grove in the foreground or middle-distance and the farther away parts of the garden are only vaguely seen the garden will seem larger because a scene through a frame of tree trunks seems farther away. This practice is distinctly different from that of most other parts of the world where shrubs and trees are banked along the property line with the tallest plants set in the rear and the shorter ones to the front. The Japanese (well aware also of plants for screening and enclosure) use the naturalistic plant groupings they have seen in nature and apply the same devices the painter uses to give perspective to a landscape painting.

In a small entrance garden where space is very limited a curved or angled path will make the front door seem farther away. The planting of low shrubbery will also increase the feeling of depth. A very gloomy effect would be created by too many and too large shrubs. The planting of a single tree in the middle of the path will obscure the view of the door and make it appear farther away.

A very important trick in making the smallest place seem uncrowded and uncontrived is to leave plenty of empty spaces. Though these empty spaces may be covered with sand or moss they are frequently absolutely bare.

Sand which is often used to symbolize the sea suggests a grand view and the expanse of land and air make the garden feel much larger than it is.

Color can be used to create illusion. Painting the walls of a garden a light color will make it appear to recede. If plants and materials of brighter shades are placed near the house and darker shades in the distance greater space will be felt.

Another type of optical illusion may be the answer. Take as an example a small plot of grass or a small sand garden laid out with the back width slightly narrower than the width near the house. The garden perspective will appear to recede faster into the distance.

Proportions are carefully figured. The spaces alloted to land and water, or water symbols, are carefully planned to present the most pleasing contrast.

38. *Vistas emphasizing the three-dimensional quality of the landscape add to the apparent size of a small garden. A common device to achieve this result is to design a garden pond on a diagonal. The snow-viewing stone lantern at the water's edge casts intriguing shadows.*

Reflections in the water of trees, rocks, clouds, sky and other objects are considered a part of the composition. The garden designer also carefully considers scale relationship between the man-made features and over-all size of the garden. A too large stone lantern, pagoda, bridge or rock arrangement in a small garden would destroy the feeling of spaciousness. If a garden feature of correct proportion and special interest is placed near the house the eyes will be occupied with the foreground and not with the background.

Japanese gardens illustrate to perfection what thoughtful planning can do for a very small space. Even in a confined space the Japanese can create an illusion of a continuous series of spaces which go beyond the actual garden structures. Zen concepts affirm the reality that infinity is ever moving with space a universal medium through which life moves in constant transformation. Time and place are only relative.

Ground Cover

A major garden problem with us is ground covers. Most of those used are fine for small areas but often not practical for use over large spaces. Therefore, grass with its expensive upkeep is depended on for use over much of the garden. Here the raked sand technique opens up new vistas in garden planning. Sand can provide an interesting, eye-soothing ground cover which will require minimum maintenance.

In narrow passages between buildings where light is poor, in situations where the soil conditions are difficult—such as under the shade of certain kinds of trees and shrubs or where root competition practically excludes all other plant growth—the garden planner can take advantage of the use of attractive and interesting arrangements of stone, pebbles or sand set off by moss. Such gardens can convey a feeling of spaciousness within a limited area by skillful use of appropriate materials.

Dry Landscape

Dry landscape, *kare-sansui*, designs and techniques have immense possibilities and these quiet gardens can play a role in the lives of all people today. Rocks and sand are the most unchanging of garden materials and require little care. Furthermore, they may be placed anywhere, even in the deep shade of tall buildings or trees or inside the buildings themselves. The Ryoanji garden has had a tremendous influence on present day Japanese and Western land-scaped gardens. Sand and stone combinations have particularly great possibilities in patio and courtyard design, not only from an aesthetic standpoint but for practical reasons as well.

But let me remind you that many gardeners with perfectly satisfactory situations will want to construct a garden based on Zen styles for the great pleasure and satisfaction such a garden can give. They may with the full freedom of an open mind combine the best of the past with design to fit the present and produce a garden of refinement and vigor.

Although water constitutes one of the chief ornaments of a good garden, natural water may not be available and city water is expensive. So water is symbolized! In dry landscape technique a water scene is portrayed with white sand or gravel and occasional rocks. These imaginary scenes are quite strongly expressed when the sand or gravel is raked into waved patterns to represent the flow of water. If light and air permit, living plants can effectively emphasize the design but if the place is too dark for plants to grow a hauntingly beautiful, waterless stream can be made from only sand and stone.

Unfortunately the average traveler to Japan sees nothing but a few external decorative elements. He does not see the modern, simply designed home gardens or the very old home gardens nor does he take the time to truly experience the ancient temple gardens. Many visitors miss the real point of a Japanese garden and think only in terms of twisted pines, Japanese cherries, unpainted wood, rocky pools, waterfalls, pagodas, stone lanterns, sand, pebbles and Buddhas. The materials of a Japanese garden are not just romantic props. The sand and stones are used for more than just easy upkeep and dramatic effect. Japanese gardens are of pure, logical and honest design, founded on universal art principles. Their elements are so arranged as to convey a feeling of the partnership of man, nature and art. A good garden has naturalness, simplicity, strength and human warmth, but above all there is a spirituality and sense of repose and meditation. Perhaps the greatest lesson we can learn from Japanese gardens is the capturing of serenity.

I am not saying that the way to peace of mind is through the gate of a Japanese garden but I do feel that we can learn much from Japan in addition to design and the handling of materials. For many years we have been preoccupied with the materialistic aspect of building "functional" gardens. Why can't we have a garden that is functional and at the same time have a place for quiet withdrawal for rest and re-creation as well as recreation? Actually, what more important function can a garden have than the renewal of mind and body through rest and mediation? Landscape designers and architects realize the depth of the need of the American people to get back to nature. This has resulted in contemporary houses and so-called indoor-outdoor living.

Living close to nature is the very essence of Japanese life. They make little distinction between nature and deity. An understanding of the attitudes and values that produced their awareness, sensitivity and know-how can help us find our own means to the same rewarding end and to a more serene way of life in troubled times.

THE JAPANESE HOUSE, A PART OF THE GARDEN

The garden is so intimately related to the house and its interior that it is impossible to discuss Japanese gardens and flower arrangement without giving some thought to the home. Japanese domestic architecture has always aimed at perfect harmony with nature and between the house and the garden. Nature endowed Japan with beautiful features and the Japanese have succeeded, to a remarkable degree, in merging the house and landscape into a true entity. Mysteriously and amazingly, the stark standardized building harmonizes with the relaxed asymmetry of the tiny, jewel-like garden and the two are completely interrelated.

The plans and layout of a Japanese house have been largely influenced by the climate and by the way in which the people live. According to custom,

39. *A Japanese garden viewed from inside the house. When the* shoji *screens are removed the garden becomes an extension of the room.*

they always remove their shoes when entering the house and sit on knees and heels on *tatami* (mats) that cover the surface of the floor or on a cushion placed on the tatami. Because no chairs are necessary, the rooms are small and the ceilings low. The design and construction are practical and architecturally beautiful. The climate of Tokyo has been compared to that of Washington, D. C.; however, I don't believe it gets as cold in Japan in winter or as hot in Washington in summer. Since the islands of Japan extend north to south, there is some climatic variation from section to section. The four seasons are clearly divided from each other and are of about equal duration. The summer months are very oppressive because of extreme humidity. Some rain falls throughout the year with a particularly rainy season from about the middle of June lasting for a month or more. The primary consideration in planning and building their homes is meeting the conditions of the summer months. Houses have few permanent walls, the external and internal divisions being formed with sliding, removable doors which permit the air to enter freely. To protect these lightly built, sliding exterior walls, the roof projects as far as possible and a veranda is built along the South side of the house to provide shade. Also, as a protection against dampness, the ground floor of the house has been traditionally built one and a half to two and a half feet above the ground on posts.

The many apertures make the house pleasant for summer living and also make house and garden flow into each other.

The layout of a typical Japanese house is comprised of three distinct parts: the raised area covered with *tatami* which includes all the living quarters; the raised area with wooden floors including the corridors, veranda and sometimes kitchen; and a small lower part at almost ground level which includes the entrance hall and sometimes the bathroom and kitchen or a section of the kitchen. The principal room is the reception room with an anteroom almost the same size connected to it by sliding doors, *fusuma*. The average size of the reception room is eight to ten mats and this with its anteroom usually serves as a guest chamber. When a large space is required for a gathering the four *fusuma* (doors) separating the reception room and anteroom can be removed. A *fusuma* is five feet ten inches high and about three feet wide and is composed of a wooden frame with several layers of heavy paper glued to it on both sides and a piece of decorative paper or a painting is laid on to cover the whole surface. A narrow frame of wood, usually lacquered black, borders the entire partition. *Fusuma* serve as doors on wall cupboards and as entrance doors also.

The refined elegance of a Japanese room emanates from its design, the beauty and charm of natural wood surfaces, the soft light transmitted through paper doors and windows, and the exquisite tone of pale green *tatami*.

On the sides of the house where there are no verandas, the openings are in the form of paper windows called elbow-rest windows because they slide on a low sill about twelve inches high and offer an unobstructed view when sitting in the Japanese manner.

The sides of the rooms that open on the veranda have sliding doors called *shoji*. These are the same size as *fusuma* and slide in grooves between the floor beam and the lintel. Both the *shoji* and the small paper windows consist of wooden frames and latticework with plain white translucent paper applied to the outside. For protection against rain and to keep out possible intruders at night *shoji* doors and windows which open directly outside where there is no closed porch have a special kind of sliding shutter called *amado* or rain door. These are bolted at night and during the day when not in use are slid into compartments at the ends of the door and window opening.

Almost every small house has a veranda facing south that serves also as a corridor. A large house often has two or more verandas in addition to one or more inside halls. A Japanese house requires a minimum of interior decoration and the arrangement of the rooms is dictated by the size of the house.

Ample storage space is one of the secrets of the uncluttered look. The clean, bare look of Japanese rooms might lead one to think that the people austerely resist possessions, but this is not the case. Actually, they own and need many changes of accessories. In a single day they may refurnish each room a number of times. Every season, every holiday, every festival day some of the furnishings must be changed. To meet the need for keeping replacements easily available they have worked out ingenious storage methods. Most-frequently-used articles are kept on shelves behind sliding doors, and many houses have special storage rooms besides.

An important type of storage room for the larger houses is the godown. This is a fireproof storehouse called the *dozo* or *kura* either attached to the house or separated from it. They are usually two-storied and have exceptionally thick walls of concrete. The thick roof is concrete as are the windows and door which swing on hinges. The earlier godowns were made of clay and when fire threatened the house, the godown windows were immediately closed and the joints and seams filled with clay which was always kept handy and ready for use.

One of the most notable characteristics of Japanese homes and gardens is serenity. This is frequently mistaken for extreme simplicity but upon deeper analysis one finds it is the product of a highly developed controlled complexity. The rather primitive-seeming simplicity does not mean that they are built with primitive methods and archaic design but in reality represents a purity of style refined through several centuries.

Perhaps to people who regard ostentation as desirable all Japanese houses look humble. The whimsical habit of some highly cultured Japanese of concealing prestige and wealth behind a humble exterior remains today as in olden times. In Japan, solitude is a status symbol. Residential streets have no sidewalks or front lawns; rather, they resemble country lanes except for the fact that they are bordered by solid fences (usually of bamboo, wood or stucco). Trees and plants peeping over give them a homey look.

Japanese architecture and gardens are storehouses of ideas for simplifying our own homes and gardens in these times of hurry and need for low maintenance. The house itself could well serve American prefabricators of modern houses as examples of attractive standardization which is acceptable to millions of people. The traditional Japanese house antedates our supposedly modern architecture by several hundred years. Skeleton structure, sliding walls and open-plan design have only in recent years been adapted by our architects. Removable walls are still in the future, as are resilient floors. All room sizes are measured by *tatami* whose dimensions never vary. Three feet wide, six feet long and at least two inches thick, they furnish a continuous floor covering which yields pleasantly underfoot. The *tatami* are made of a finely woven rush mounted on a rice straw body about two inches thick with a black fabric binding on the long side. The garden as a visual wall of a room is also a relatively new idea in America. It has been employed in Japan for at least a thousand years! When sliding walls are removed in hot weather the garden and house become truly integrated.

The Japanese house has a message for us in the Western world in the way it can be manipulated. As mentioned earlier room sizes can be changed by opening the sliding doors. Outside walls can be removed or manipulated in a variety of ways for changing weather and social requirements. The three by six feet *tatami* governs not only the dimensions of a room (whose size is always a multiple of a *tatami*) but also those of the sliding partitions and walls of the house, the movable chests and the built-in shelves and drawers. This is true of every dimension of the houses at every level of society from the poor farmer's hut to the palatial house of a wealthy manufacturer.

A room is often refurnished several times each day depending on the events to take place. No room is set aside for only one specific function. Any room can be used for sleeping, eating, working or playing.

Our accommodations in a Japanese inn consisted at night of a reception-room, bedroom and dressingroom. By day beds were stored in closets, the screens pushed back or removed and it became one large room which could accommodate a very large luncheon or dinner party. There was always a fresh flower arrangement in the *tokonoma* and by opening the *shoji* screens on the south side the garden became a part of our lovely quarters.

Japanese houses look flimsy to Westerners, but actually they are very sturdily built and have many extra supports to make them earthquake proof and able to withstand the violent typhoons which sweep the country from time to time. The roof of the average Japanese house is quite solid with thick, well-baked and often gracefully curved tiles. I have never seen wooden houses in any other part of the world with roofs built in such elaborate and substantial designs.

Japan lies at a latitude from 38 to 45 degrees north, almost the same as Northern California and extends as far south as Spain and Portugal in Europe. Situated as it is and in addition having its shores washed by the warm Japan Current one would suppose that Japan would be much warmer in winter than it really is. Bleak cold wind from the Siberian wilderness sweeps down and this coupled with dampness produces a very penetrating coldness. However, the sky is usually very clear and bright in winter and the sun is quite warm. Therefore, Japanese houses are constructed to take in as much sunshine as possible. Each house has a spacious veranda facing south so as to obtain a maximum of the sun's warmth. In sections that are particularly windy in winter, farmhouses have very tall hedges growing at the back, or north side, of the houses to shelter them from the wind and cold.

Heating

The traditional Japanese home has no central heating but is heated in the traditional manner with a charcoal burner or brazier called a *hibachi*. The Japanese must dress warmly since they are able to warm only their hands over the charcoal burner. The famous Japanese steaming hot bath is a marvelous warmer-upper! We visited in a Japanese inn one cold February and it is surprising how long a good hot bath will keep you warm and cozy. If you visit Japan in winter do carry your shoes in with you at night so that you can warm them the next morning. Shoes left at the entrance will be icy.

TOKONOMA

The *tokonoma* is the most important feature of a Japanese house and is always found in the principal room of even the simplest traditional home. In a large house there will perhaps be two or more. A *tokonoma* is a recessed alcove which is a kind of shrine dedicated to the exercise of aesthetic sensitivity. It is never crowded. Three objects and no more are allowed at one time: a *kakemono* (scroll painting), a flower arrangement and a small metal or porcelain ornament (usually an incense burner). Often only the flower arrangement and *kakemono* are displayed. Monotony is avoided by frequently changing these ornaments and interest is stimulated by the timeliness of the objects used and the appropriateness of the flower arrangement. The *kakemono* is changed to conform to the season, to observe certain festivals and holidays and for the simple pleasure of enjoying another scroll. A cultured Japanese family may possess a large number of *kakemonos* acquired through many generations of art collecting. Those not in use are rolled up, placed in especially made individual boxes and kept in cupboards or fireproof godowns as are the other art objects that are placed one at a time in the *tokonoma*.

Priests in Zen monasteries are credited with having originated the *tokonoma* during medieval times when they hung Buddhist pictures on the wall behind a low stand on which was placed a vase of flowers, a candlestick and an incense burner. However, some scholars trace its origin to more ancient times and Shinto religion. It was originally the bed place reserved for *kami* and later a place of honor for the "superior" to sit and view the garden. At any rate, it was the Zen Buddhist alcove arrangement which became the prototype of the secular *tokonoma*. The early *tokonoma* in domestic dwellings was actually a family altar on which was placed an image of Buddha and an offering of flowers and burning incense. The whole family gathered before this altar in the mornings and evenings to worship. Today the religious significance has dimmed but the Japanese still retain a feeling of sacredness toward this alcove. Nothing unclean or untidy is ever placed in it—only things of meaning and beauty.

40. *The* tokonoma, *a recessed alcove, is the most important feature of a traditional Japanese house and is always in the principal room of even the simplest home. This drawing shows a* tokonoma *containing a hanging scroll,* kakemono, *and a classical arrangement of aspidistra leaves. Sometimes a small incense burner or other art object is also placed in the* tokonoma.

床に軸物花取り合せ　葉らんを床に挿る節は
軸物に色彩あるものか、又一行書などが適す。

Even though the *tokonoma* now gratifies only an aesthetic sense there seems to be an awareness of the original religious ideals that resulted in the efforts of the people to bring the earthly life as close as possible to that of the other world that existed in their imagination and heart.

Etiquette for Viewing a *Tokonoma* Arrangement

There is a certain etiquette observed in viewing a flower arrangement in a *tokonoma* as there is with everything else in the daily life of the Japanese people. When a guest enters a room he should advance to within about three feet of the *tokonoma* and kneel on the *tatami*. From this position with his hands on the mat he bows first to the host and then to the *tokonoma* in recognition of the effort the host has made to interpret a work of art. Next he should look at the *kakemono*. After a pause in appreciation his eyes move to the flower arrangement. He views first the *shin* stem, then the *soe* and *tai* and finally the container and stand. If there is another object of art in the *tokonoma* this is admired too. It should be remembered that it is the art with which the flowers are arranged that is important, not the flowers themselves. After properly complimenting his host on his cleverness in choosing the scroll and designing the flower arrangement, the guest should bow again, this time in thanks, before he fits quietly into the home setting.

The Western visitor need not be concerned about observing the precise Japanese procedure in viewing the *tokonoma*. It is not expected of you. A quiet, gracious, respectful and genuine appreciation of the efforts of your host is all that is necessary.

Tokonoma vary in size, form and arrangement of details depending on the structure of the room and the direction from which the light filters in. It is never placed in the center of a wall due to the fact that rooms are designed asymmetrically. Because of the custom of keeping all household objects stored away in closets, the average Japanese room is usually no more than twelve by fifteen feet. A room of that size will have an alcove six feet wide by three feet deep. A large room may have an alcove double that size. The floor of a *tokonoma* is raised a few inches above room level and is either of polished boards or *tatami*. On one side may be a *shoin* and on the other a post of ornamental wood and a partition next to which is the *tana*.

Tana and *Shoin*

Next to the *tokonoma* in importance are the *tana* (or *chigai-dana*) and the *shoin* which give the room a variety of interesting arrangements and are in reality a part of the *tokonoma*.

The *tana* or *chigai-dana* is a recess next to the *tokonoma* artistically designed with shelves arranged stepwise and small cupboards. It is sometimes called *tokowaki* which means beside the *tokonoma.* Its purpose is to provide variation in the architecture of the room and to display art objects.

The term *shoin* was originally applied to a bay window with a wide sill used for reading and writing in the dwelling of Zen priests. Later when *shoin* was developed as part of the architecture of a home the term was applied to any area having such a window. The *shoin* is a beautiful decorative interior feature and is placed next to and at right angles to the *tokonoma.*

The *tokonoma* design depends on the structure of the room, the position of the garden and the direction from which light comes into the room. If light comes from the right as one faces the *tokonoma,* the *shoin* is to the right and the *tana* to the left. If the light comes from the left the position is reversed.

The *tokonoma* is the point of focus in the room and has been compared to the fireplace in a Western room since the fireplace forms a center of interest and serves also as an important decoration. Just as people in the West invite friends to the fireside for pleasure and hospitality, the people of this island country have guests sit before the *tokonoma* and entertain them with a picture and flower arrangement and offer their own brand hospitality.

We see more and more Oriental influence in modern interior decoration. Many Westerners have acquired Chinese and Japanese hanging scrolls. These are charming and can provide a perfect setting for a flower arrangement when hung over an appropriate chest or table.

How to Use a *Kakemono*

Although in using a *kakemono* in a Western home we need not be severely restricted, it will help us if we keep in mind a few points relative to the Japanese way of using a *kakemono.*

Remember a *tokonoma* grouping is never crowded—a wall-hanging, a flower arrangement and a small art object or incense burner and nothing more! Often there is only the *kakemono* and flower arrangement. In any case all elements are complementary to each other. The scroll sets the style and mood and is the inspiration for the flower arrangement. Unifying the two requires an understanding of the relationship between the context of the scroll and the flower arrangement and container. There are two types of *kakemono*: calligraphy called *kakeji* and paintings called *kakezu.* The motif of a picture is not duplicated in the arrangement. A technique so obvious is monotonous. When the picture represents a certain flower or tree it is better to avoid using the same plant material for your arrangement. If the picture is richly colored simple leaves or white flowers are preferable. Be careful also that the color of your flowers is not the same as that of the marginal cloth or paper of the hanging scroll. In Japanese interior decoration reiteration is useless and meaningless because every form and

41. *A traditional* tatami-*matted Japanese room is being made ready for tea. In the* tokonoma *hangs a* kakemono, *hanging scroll, with a flower arrangement to the right.*

color must have its own reason for being. They make an exception when a calligraphy poem extols the beauty of a certain flower or tree.

The artist's seal on a *kakemono* is never obscured by the flowers for this would be rude to the painter or calligrapher.

When people are pictured care must be taken not to shade the faces of the persons in the picture.

If guests are invited the *kakemono* must be in accord with the time of day. In the daytime a finely drawn picture or scroll of small characters will be acceptable, but in the evening you should choose a clearly drawn or painted picture or a calligraphic hanging with broad, clear characters written in a single line.

Consider a very obvious example of a harmonious combination: If your wall-hanging represents a waterfall, the flower arrangement must consist of flowers that grow in or near water and the ornament must be a bronze or porcelain fish, fisherman or some object that is closely associated with water. Volumes could be written along this line and a well-designed flower arrangement in Japan never errs in this regard. It seems impossible for the Japanese to enjoy flowers just as flowers. There is hardly a plant that does not have some metaphysical or historical association—often both. Certain combinations are recognized by all as suggesting a tradition, a season of the year, a poem or an emotion. In both art and literature flowers are a favorite motif and are often associated with certain birds and animals.

See the chapter on symbolism for other associations.

The *tokonoma* is a result, not a cause, of flower arrangement. In our homes we have places for arrangements that are just as definite as the *tokonoma* where we have planned backgrounds against which we enjoy our flowers. My favorite places in our home are the dining-room table, a chest over which hangs a portrait, my desk and the stand before a *kakemono* in my study. My husband has a favorite place in his office too and often filches my arrangements and transfers them to a chest there. Only a Japanese arrangement could span the gulf between a traditional 18th century home and a modern business office.

OTHER FEATURES

Family Altars

Still preserved in most Japanese homes is the ancient tradition of both Shinto and Buddhist deities venerated in miniature family altars placed in one or two of the principal rooms. Though both Shinto and Buddhist altars are found in the same house there is no religious conflict. Each member of the family can worship at both altars without any compunction whatever. There is a clear distinction between Shintoism and Buddhism in their sphere of influence and function.

Shinto Family Altar, *Kamidana* or God-Shelf

The original Japanese religion was an unorganized worship of nature and the spirits of the dead which developed through the centuries into a native Shinto cult. As a religion it is concerned with a variety of deities known as *kami* which vary in nature from the spirits of trees, rocks, flowers, mountains, seas, fire, winds and all kinds of birds and animals to deified ancestors, heros, emperors and a pantheon of heavenly deities chief among whom is the Sun Goddess. The worship of such things is an expression of the belief that objects of nature have indwelling souls.

Household Shinto ceremonies are, as would be expected, centered around family matters such as anniversaries of the deaths of relatives and ancestors and the birth and naming of a child. A miniature shrine (which can be purchased in any shopping district in Japan) is usually placed in the principal room on a board shelf high up in the corner of the room perhaps above a closet door. This small shrine is referred to as a god-shelf or *kamidana*. Within it are sacred tablets, one for the Grand Shrine of Ise and one for the tutelary shrine. There may be memorial tablets for deceased relatives hanging just below and perhaps to one side of the altar. In the front of the god-shelf is a tiny stand for an offering and at either side there may be a candle. In the large homes of the old families the *kamidana* are frequently handsome architectural reproductions of Shinto shrines and measure as much as six feet in height.

The earnest Shintoist will rise in the morning, perform his ablutions, and then step in front of the shrine, bow, clap his hands twice, bow for a moment in silence, and then depart, ready to face the day. On special occasions he will purify himself by bathing and perhaps add a cold plunge for simple austerity; then standing before the shrine he will further purify himself by waving over each shoulder a branch of camellia-like *sakaki* tree, *Eurya ochnacea,* the sacred tree of Shinto. Small bottles of *sake* are offered to the deities.

Sometimes a home will have a small shrine in the garden where these observances take place. The worshipper will step into the garden, face the rising sun, a mountain, Ise, or some other sacred place, clap his hands, and then bow for a moment in silence.

Buddhist Family Altar, *Butsudan*

In contrast to the Shinto altar, which is plain and bare of ornaments, the *Butsudan* is usually decorated with rich carvings and fine lacquer work. The altar has in its sanctuary a statue of Buddha and tablets bearing the posthumus Buddhist names of deceased members of the family. Posthumus name means one given every Buddhist believer after death. In old families with long histories these tablets may span centuries.

Every morning a pair of candles are lighted on the family altars and each member of the family worships before them. A bell on the Buddhist altar is rung every time respect is paid the departed. The light of the candles should not be blown out with the mouth but waved out by hand. If good fortune of any kind visits the family, it is reported to the altars. Every gift of food (except fish and meat) has to be offered to the altar before it is eaten. A small bowl of boiled rice and sometimes fruits, sweets or vegetables are offered each morning to the deceased members. These offerings signify that the departed spirits are still considered among the members of the family and are respectfully greeted with a reverent "good morning."

Other Furnishings

A low table is the most common piece of movable furniture found in a Japanese room. It serves many purposes, especially as a dining table when the traditional *ozen* (individual trays) are not used.

An article frequently used to embellish the room is a characteristic Japanese folding screen called a *byobu* or a single-panel screen called a *tsuitate*.

There are sometimes a few movable chests and cupboards in the living room but these are limited in size due to the many built-in cupboards and drawers.

For sleeping a *futon* or *toko* is brought out from a wall cupboard and spread on the *tatami*. The *futon* is a mattress of wadded cotton an inch or so thick on which is placed a pillow and a quilted coverlet. In a deluxe Japanese inn we found the *futon* made of foam rubber and heated with a bed-size electric heating pad! They were deliciously comfortable.

The *futon* is a marvelous idea for a holiday house. Imagine how many you could sleep in a small area and the fun of sleeping on the floor—particularly for children and teenagers. A room or two with lots of *futon*, a large *hibachi* or two for cooking the food and you have the setting for a delightful house-party. Many years ago when we built our river house we designed it in the manner of a mountain cabin. If we were building a holiday house today it would be patterned after a traditional Japanese house.

BONKEI, BONSEKI
AND BONSAI
IV

Bonkei and *bonseki* are much alike in that both of these two miniature arts of Japan consist of creating small landscapes or waterscapes on trays. Broadly speaking, both may be termed tray landscapes. The essential difference between the two is the materials used. *Bonkei* literally means "tray landscape" and is made of stones, earth, and tiny plants. *Bonseki* means "tray stone" and the materials required are stones, pebbles and sand. Both *bonkei* and *bonseki* are comparatively easy and anyone can make them with fair success. These are ideal hobbies for the apartment dweller or anyone who has the desire to create garden scenes but does not have the space.

Tray landscapes are attractive home ornaments both for Western and Japanese rooms. The Japanese use them in the *tokonoma* but they are charming anywhere that you would use a flower arrangement. They are particularly well suited for table decoration when made to be viewed from all sides.

In ancient times appreciation of natural stones placed on a cushion of gold brocade, a red sandalwood base or a tray was widespread among court nobles, aristocrats and Buddhist priests. The taste gradually became popular with the general public and eventually plants, trees and sand or small gravel came to be used with the stones to make miniature garden landscapes which sprang from their imagination.

In Japan there are schools for teaching the arts of *bonkei* and *bonseki*, but anyone with a knowledge of good design can construct charming landscape scenes by applying the same principles that are employed in making a garden, flower arrangement, or *bonsai*.

101

42. (Above) This bonkei *portrays a mountain rising steeply from the sea. Two islands are joined to the mainland by gently arching bridges.*

43. (Below) *A rectangular lacquer tray holds a scene of Mt. Fuji. In the foreground are picturesque small pine trees growing beside the sea.*

Stones, sand and tiny plants collected during an outing at the seashore, lake or river can contribute a sentimental as well as practical aspect to the making of a tray landscape.

To heighten perspective and interest miniature ornaments such as houses, bridges, pagodas, lanterns, boats, etc. are often added but this can easily be overdone. A well-done *bonkei* or *bonseki* needs little or no embellishment.

BONKEI

Bonkei, landscapes in trays, is an art form somewhat more realistic and less abstract than *bonseki* and is a miniature copy of mother nature. Oval or rectangular trays which measure one to three feet long by one-half to one and one-half feet wide are generally used.

The contemporary art of tray landscape is divided into two groups. One is the classic *bonkei* in which natural stones are used with trees, grasses, sand and the like as found in nature, to create realistic, three dimensional landscape scenes. The other method is to model mountains, rocks, ocean waves, and other elements of a scene from special kinds of clay. These are painted in natural colors and powdered moss is sprinkled on to provide the textures of vegetation. Tiny trees and natural, dried, or artificial grasses and plant materials may be used. By using artificial materials the Japanese have been able to preserve their *bonkei* work and transport it to other countries and in this way *bonkei* is becoming known throughout the world. But I much prefer the use of natural materials and feel that the classical use of beautiful stones with fresh, growing plants and mosses is in better taste for use in our homes. These long-lasting tray designs can serve as charming additions to any room. If the plants are well chosen and cared for they will need to be repotted only every two or three years at which time it may be necessary to separate and rearrange the different plants.

Planting a Bonkei

The tray or container should not be more than two inches deep and care should be taken not to try to work in too much material just because it is attractive. It is better to discard an interesting rock in favor of a smaller, duller one if the former would overpower the tray and make the plants look cramped. Avoid also the temptation to use a decorative plant or tree that is too large as the resulting lack of proportion will grow more and more evident as the plant grows. In making a *bonkei,* as in designing a garden, making a flower arrangement or a *bonsai,* never forget that empty spaces form an extremely important part of the pattern so do not overcrowd it.

44. *(Above) This bonkei was designed to be seen from all sides and is suitable for a table. Note the beautifully gnarled pine tree so typical of Japan.*

45. *(Below) Landscape showing a stream gushing from a large rock.*

There is almost no combination of plants which with imagination and inventiveness cannot be made into an interesting and effective group landscape planting. The gardener is limited only by the bounds of his creativeness and a few practical, common-sense considerations. For instance it is not sensible to combine plants which require different soils and care such as cactus with alpine plants. All the plants for a group planting should be collected before-hand along with all the other materials and tools for planting the landscape. A safe rule to follow in choosing the soil is to reproduce as closely as possible the soil found in the plants' native habitat. A sticky peat mixture will be needed for use with rocks. Growing moss will be needed for ground-cover.

To plant fill the tray three quarters full of soil and if rocks are to be used place them next and anchor them with clay or peat. There should always be some one focal point or main plant, perhaps even an actual *bonsai*, while the rest of the plantings consisting of secondary plants and ground cover will be chosen to complement this keynote. Trees, always uneven in number, may dot the landscape and be bunched slightly about a third of the width across to make a focal point. The focal point is very important as it prevents the plant-ing from looking dull and monotonous. The area can be built up to form a hill or a slope or rocks can be used to give emphasis. Trees or shrubs can be planted on a nucleus of peat behind the rocks. A level stretch of sand or fine gravel to simulate a pool or a stream balances the trees effectively. When everything is in place soil should be poured in to almost fill the tray and dampened moss can be pressed with the fingers into areas where a ground cover is needed. When the planting is complete it should be watered carefully.

Imagine this beautiful *bonkei* suitable for a patio or terrace made in a long, narrow tray or trough. Two thirds of the surface is taken up by an uneven bank of soil and rocks planted with trees and shrubs while the remaining third in the foreground is a level "river" of sand! What could be more picturesque and charming?

BONSEKI

Bonseki, the art of stone and sand, is more abstract than *bonkei*. It is an art which consists of portraying a landscape or seascape artistically on a black rectangular or oval lacquered tray or board with white sand and stones. The result is a spectacular contrast of sparkling white sand on a black tray with the symbolic expression and simple beauty of an ink painting. The most popular tray is of black-lacquered wood one to two feet long, one half to one foot wide and one half inch deep. A handsome lacquer tray can become the canvas of a thousand paintings that can be changed according to mood and season. One can suggest a rising sun, a full moon, bright rays of sunshine, angry waves dashing against rocks, a babbling stream, a waterfall, white sailboats floating

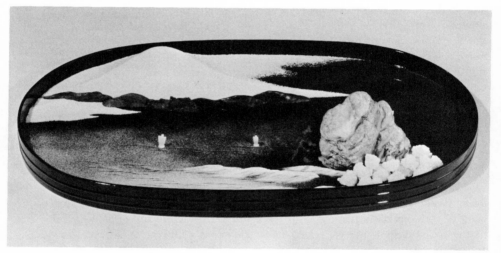

46. *(Above) Gentle waves wash the shore of a rocky island.*

47. *(Below) A winter day! Rolling mountains rise in the distance behind rocky fields. This arrangement would be suitable for the center of a table.*

on a calm sea, a landscape covered with mist and clouds or a myriad of other scenes.

Stones of all shapes (some fantastically formed) are used to represent mountain ranges or islands. Coarse sand is used to portray villages, fine sand suggests mist, clouds, rain, the sea and distant mountains, and other grades of sand form trees and other scenery. This is a wonderful way to use and admire particularly fine stones. The blackness of the tray and the stones make an elegant contrast with the whiteness of the sand. In Japan some *bonseki* stones have come down from generation to generation as prized art treasures.

The tools used for this art consist of feathers of various kinds; stencils to shape the moon and sun; thin rectangular boards to form the horizon, mist, and rainfall; spoons of different shapes to deposit the graded sand onto the board; sifting screens to produce tonal qualities of shading and for grading the sand; and chopsticks for picking up and arranging very coarse sand and removing or rearranging pieces without disturbing the others.

Some *bonseki* artists use colored sands to represent water, the rising sun, etc. but white sand is the most popular and is considered in better taste.

Recently a method of preserving certain types of *bonseki* by mixing sand with pulverized glue and making it adhere to the lacquered tray by a steaming process has been developed, but the Japanese prefer the perishable nature of a traditional sand painting where only sand and rocks and sometimes ornaments are used.

Tray landscapes, like flower arranging and gardening, were developed and refined by Zen priests along with the tea ceremony. The chief aim of Zen is to calm and concentrate the mind so it can be spiritually awakened so it is natural that devotees turn to the garden, a composition in space, in their meditation. The dominating feature in gardens based on Zen ideas are the stones and they are of more interest than trees and plants. The most famous Zen garden is the stone garden at Ryoanji Temple. This garden is said to have been designed by a Zen priest and the idea and much of the form was borrowed from *bonseki*.

The stone garden at Ryoanji is a small flat garden surrounded by an earthen wall. There are no trees, plants or accessories—only fifteen stones arranged in five groups on a ground of white sand. It could be called a *bonseki* garden. The stones symbolize islands, the sand the sea, and all are in beautiful harmony with the space in which it is composed. In the same way *bonseki* often symbolizes islands with stones and the sea with silver sand. The only difference is that *bonseki* is presented in a tray. Such symbolic simplicity is the way of expression of which the Japanese are so fond.

BONSAI

Bonsai (pronounced bone-sigh) is a Japanese art in which the beautiful forms of large mature trees are captured in dwarfed plants. Three feet is generally considered the maximum size. The word bonsai means tray tree and is becoming well-known in many countries outside Japan. The art of growing and caring for dwarfed trees may be enjoyed practically anywhere in the world. Men are particularly intrigued with the art.

48. *This Japanese red pine was collected from a mountainside in Japan more than one hundred years ago.*

Bonsai are not dwarfed by heredity. They are cultural dwarfs. We see trees growing in rocky crevices on the mountain side or along storm swept coasts that have been buffeted by wind and weather. In their struggle for life against adversity they often acquire a charm rarely seen in trees growing in more fertile and peaceful surroundings. Some of these have lived for a century or more and are still only a few feet high. When such trees are grown in appropriate containers they are a form of living art appreciated by all who love and understand nature. These are the bonsai of Japan that are common all over the country and used for decorative and exhibition purposes.

History

The early history of the cultivation and appreciation of bonsai is a disputed subject. The oldest authentic record of bonsai is pictures of dwarfed trees in containers on a scroll written in 1310. In all probability during the sixteenth century when flower arrangement, gardens, and tea ceremony achieved such exquisite perfection bonsai gained the status of an established art also. By the nineteenth century the art had reached the pinnacle of perfection that it enjoys today.

At first bonsai were owned only by nobles and members of the wealthy merchant class who could afford rare things. But as the idea of artificially improving the shape of potted trees grew and as the Japanese began to realize that it would be possible to create dwarfs artificially in quantity from seeds and cuttings the use of bonsai became more general. These are as beautiful as very ancient naturally stunted potted trees that were collected and treasured. They have a convincing naturalness that rivals nature. The Japanese enhance the plants' essential beauty without corruption or distortion. Their aim is not to make a plant freakish or grotesque.

BONSAI IN AMERICA As information concerning bonsai has become readily available in this country more and more people are adopting this fascinating hobby. Bonsai clubs are springing up in various sections. There is a large

49. *(Left) A bonsai of golden larch about twenty years old is pictured in winter conditions after needles have fallen.*

50. *(Right) A bonsai shop in Kyoto displays its wares.*

concentration of interest and nice bonsai collections on the west coast particularly in the Los Angeles and San Francisco areas. In Boston at the Arnold Arboretum the Larz Anderson collection, which contains some of the oldest specimen bonsai in the country, has attracted much attention. The Brooklyn Botanic Garden in New York has a very extensive collection of many species, some of which are quite rare specimens of the art of dwarfed trees. Each year Brooklyn Botanic Garden offers courses in bonsai for both beginners and advance groups. They are open to members of the Garden and everyone who may be interested. These courses include demonstrations of methods of potting, training and care of bonsai followed by actual practice.

Naturally more attention is focused on bonsai in those areas where there are collections to be viewed. However, individuals and small groups who are not near a center are experimenting and learning on their own through reading and sometimes traveling distances to further their knowledge.

Choosing Bonsai

Most bonsai are, simply stated, out-of-doors potted trees or shrubs that generally require some protection from weather extremes. In cold climates winter protection of a deep cold frame or cool greenhouse is ideal for hardy species. In hot climates emphasis is on summer protection which can be a lathe house, the shade of a tree or the wall of a terrace or the lee side of the house. In selecting bonsai varieties that will remain healthy with a minimum of special attention there are two ways of approach. First and easiest is to select plants adapted to the particular climate of your area. A second and harder way is to modify the environment and climate to meet the needs of the plants. Of course there are limits to these modifications but they are possible to a certain extent with portable plants in containers.

Species that require a cold dormant period are not adaptable to tropical areas such as Florida, Hawaii, the Rio Grande Valley in Texas and the warmer parts of California. However, the wealth of less common ornamental plants that are possible bonsai subjects more than makes up for the elimination of a few popular species.

Special restrictions will be required of bonsai growers who grow bonsai in apartments and whose access to the out-of-doors may be only a fire escape or roof garden. Difficult problems of environment and climatic conditions have been solved with ingenuity by bonsai growers in various parts of this country.

By choosing plants adaptable to the particular climate and practicing common sense, hobbyists have found the effective care of bonsai neither seriously complicated nor overly simple.

The great things to remember in choosing plants for bonsai is that to achieve satisfactory results you must choose varieties with small leaves and particularly small flowers and fruits. The tree can be dwarfed by pruning and even the leaves will become smaller with years of restricted growth, but flowers and fruit remain proportionate to the species.

Ways of Securing Plants

There are several different ways of securing bonsai plants. The most exciting way is collecting natural dwarfs. They can be found on a mountain or on the seashore where the soil is poor and strong winds distort the trunk. In Japan these are the most highly prized and the sport of the hunt itself is a very pleasant pastime. Wild seedlings can also be collected and trained. They are particularly good in group plantings. Very early spring is the best season for collecting natural dwarfs. Carry with you some good tools for digging (I like a small pick that we bought at an army surplus store) and wet sphagnum moss and plastic sheeting. It is important to retain as much soil as possible when digging a plant and try not to cut the taproot. If this is unavoidable cut the root as long as possible. Cover the earth and roots with wet sphagnum moss, spray the foilage with water and wrap securely in a plastic sheet to prevent drying out. Plant in a training pot as soon as you return, keep in a shady place, and water the roots and spray the foliage three or four times a day for the first three or four months. At the end of the first year transplant into a suitable bonsai pot. When the tree is well established branches can be wired and shaped.

Ordinary nursery stock can be purchased, pruned and trained into bonsai. This offers a vast field of plants with which one may pioneer in bonsai culture.

Bonsai of any species can be grown from seed although this method takes the most time. They may also be made from cuttings, graftings, layerings or divisions.

There are those who want to buy the finished bonsai. Such bonsai can be kept in perfect condition only by a professional bonsai grower or an experienced hobbyist. However, there is no reason why an unexperienced person cannot care for a ready-made bonsai successfully provided he has the desire to learn and can take it from time to time to a nursery or an experienced bonsai grower for advice and help.

A Few Suggested Plants for Bonsai

Acer (Japanese maple and other small-leaved kinds)
Azalea (use only small-leaved, low-growing kinds such as the Kurumes and the Satsukis)
Berberis verruculosa (Warty barberry)
Buxus microphylla compacta (Dwarf box)
Cedrus atlantica (Atlas cedar)
Chaenomeles lagenaria (Flowering quince)

Chamaecyparis (Hinoki cypress and others)
Cotoneaster (Rockspray and other varieties)
Cryptomeria japonica
Daphne odora
Gardenia radicans
Ginkgo biloba (Maidenhair tree)
Ilex (Several varieties including *Helleri,* Japanese holly)
Juniperus (Junipers in many varieties)
Lagerstroemia indica (Crepe myrtle)
Malus Sargentii (Cargent crab-apple)
Nandina domestica
Picea (Spruces in the dwarf varieties)
Pieris japonica
Pinus parviflora (Japanese white pine)
Prunus subhirtella pendula (Japanese weeping cherry)
Prunus Mume (Japanese apricot)
Pyracantha (Coccinea and *Koidzumii)*
Punica Granatum nana (Dwarf pomegranate)
Wisteria (Several varieties)
Zelkova serrata (Gray-bark elm)

Containers

Choosing the container for a bonsai plant is second only in importance to selecting and training the tree itself. As in flower arrangement an appropriate container will help make even mediocre material show off to good advantage while a poorly chosen one will destroy the effectiveness of an outstanding plant. The container (as in a flower arrangement) is an integral part of the finished composition and must be in good proportion with the plant. It must provide a base solid enough in feeling to satisfy the eye yet must not make the tree itself seem too small. Generally eighty percent tree and twenty percent container is the ideal artistic proportion between tree and container. For low-spreading trees or shrubs the plant can be sixty percent and container forty percent but in general smaller containers are better.

In a round or square pot the plant is placed in the center except for cascade styles which are planted toward the rim. In a shallow oblong or elliptical container the tree should be planted off-center at a point seventy percent of the distance from right or left end depending on the shape and spread of the branches. The lines and shape of the container should be simple and complement the tree. Fussy shapes and colors are distracting and undesirable.

Pottery containers are the ones commonly used. They may be glazed or unglazed on the outside but all are unglazed on the inside. They must have one or more holes in the bottom for drainage. Aquatic plants or trees growing with their roots entirely confined to soil on a stone are exceptions. They require a container without holes and it should be glazed on the inside.

The most desirable colors are the subdued earthy ones such as grays, greens, browns and off-whites. Sometimes blue containers are used to set off the colors of azalea blooms and some of the yellow-flowered or yellow-fruited trees. Deep red hues are lovely with white-flowered plants.

Importers are bringing in more and more bonsai pots from Japan. These may be purchased from dealers in Oriental goods and from some nursery specialists.

Care

The care of a prize bonsai has been compared to that of a prize poodle. Both require constant attention, regular clippings, daily grooming and a tonic from time to time. No one should own either a bonsai or a dog unless he is prepared to see that they are given a certain amount of care every day. Like a dog a bonsai cannot be left to look after itself if the owner goes away. If you go away for a week-end arrangements must be made to have a trustworthy person water it regularly and be sure it is in a shelter so that a sudden storm will not damage it. If you plan to be away for some time it is better to board the tree with a good nursery. If the nurseryman is not familiar with bonsai practices be sure to leave concise instructions with him.

The everyday essentials for a healthy bonsai are sun, water, air and a temperature that is not extreme. A true bonsai is a miniature forest tree, not a hothouse plant and it must live out-of-doors. It will die if kept indoors too much, especially in an overheated room. It can safely be brought in several times a week for a few hours at a time provided the room is not overheated in winter and is well ventilated in summer. If you have several bonsai you can display them in rotation and avoid the temptation to keep one indoors too much.

DISPLAYING BONSAI IN THE HOME The Japanese display a bonsai in the *toko-noma* of the principal room of the house very much as they do a flower arrangement. A bonsai always stands on a base and is never displayed alone. It is accompanied by a hanging scroll (*kakemono*) and a second smaller bonsai or an ornament. The second bonsai should contrast with the first, that is, a single specimen tree is set off by a small herb or rock planting. A fine rock or a piece of carving is often substituted for the second bonsai. If a number of miniature bonsai are displayed instead of a specimen tree they are placed on a tiered stand.

The same care goes into choosing a *kakemono* for a bonsai as for a flower arrangement. If the bonsai is elaborate the scroll is a simple short poem in calligraphy. If the scroll is of particular importance the bonsai must blend and not detract.

We can effectively display a bonsai in the same places we customarily use flowers in our homes. A good bonsai makes an elegant decoration for the dining room table.

Placement

A bonsai is a dwarf forest tree, not a hothouse plant, and should be kept out-of-doors where there is shade in summer and protection from drying winds in winter. A table or bench placed under a shade tree is an excellent spot during hot weather but the best type of shelter from sun is a lath house or something similar. Of course there are variations in the needs of different kinds of plants and in different climates.

Most bonsai can withstand freezing temperatures but one must take measures to protect and shelter them according to the variety. Prolonged exposure to freezing weather causes the moisture in the soil to turn to ice and the expansion breaks the container. One method is to bring the tree to a cool, well-lighted spot (not warmer than fifty degrees) inside the house during heavy freezes and then return it to the outside whenever feasible.

A deep cold-frame sunk below frost line affords excellent winter protection. Gravel should be placed in the bottom to provide good drainage and plants should be watered as needed. Be sure to open the sash of the cold-frame in bright weather and watch plants to be sure they do not overheat. Another idea is to bury the container in a compost which will generate heat. This should be done under a tree or next to a building where it will be sheltered from drying winds.

Tropical plants require a cool greenhouse. If care is taken to provide sufficient ventilation and prevent overheating the cool greenhouse is fine for most hardy plants as well. Few plants actually require freezing weather although they do need a cold period for normal dormancy. A temperature range of forty to fifty degrees for two to four months is usually adequate.

Elaborate, expensive equipment is not necessary. Put your ingenuity to work. You may be able to simply plant your pots in a bed and cover them with pine needles or work out some other simple shelter. Talk to bonsai fanciers and visit bonsai nurseries and you will be able to plan a routine to fit your climate and type of plants.

Adequate Water

A bonsai cannot be overwatered as long as the water can drain through the soil and out the drainage holes in the bottom of the container. More trees die from lack of water than any other cause. For only a few trees a rubber syringe with a spray head will do the job, but if there are many a garden hose with an adjustable spray nozzle is effective and expedient. Be sure the spray does not wash away the soil from the plant. The tree should generally be watered thoroughly once a day and more frequently when temperatures are high and humidity is low and during periods of rapid growth. There are of course variations in the needs of different species of plants. Common sense and experience will help simplify the routine.

In addition to watering the roots it is also essential that the leaves be sprayed to keep the foliage clean and to discourage scales and pests.

Pests and Diseases

Bonsai are susceptible to all the pests and diseases peculiar to their species when grown in normal size. However, when plants are given adequate light and air, syringed with water regularly, and general cleanliness is practiced, most trouble can be avoided. A keen watch should be kept for the first signs of any pests which will be easy to halt in the beginning.

Plants on raised benches or tables are removed from many crawling insects and an insecticide spray will handle those that might reach them. Spray all trees and shrubs in the garden near the bonsai against insects and it is a good idea to spray the ground area where the plants are kept and under the plant benches with a solution of chlordane to eliminate crawling pests such as ants that may carry aphids and sometimes diseases.

In some areas a definite program of spraying or dusting is necessary to control pests or diseases of certain kinds. Information on this can be obtained from experienced gardeners or nurserymen in your locality. There are many effective, easy to use prepared mixtures on the market. Some of the excellent ones contain combinations of malathion, DDT, lindane, and other compounds as well as the new systemic insecticides.

The beginner should be warned about some pests that might not be noticed until considerable damage has been done. Spider mites are about the size of a pinpoint and difficult to see. They may be detected by holding a white paper under the foliage and shaking the branch. The tiny insects can be seen moving about on the paper and will leave a smear when rubbed with the finger. They cause the foliage to take on a yellowish tinge and finally turn brown. When damage has advanced this far it will take some time for the plant to regain its normal healthy color. They should be sprayed or dusted several times to destroy the spiders. Sulphur dust, nicotine, parathion, and other dusts and sprays are recommended.

Scale insects are also difficult to control. They are found on the branches and leaves and look like small brown or black shells or lumps. Several sprayings may be necessary to get rid of them. Heavy scale infestations kill branches or entire trees or shrubs. Standard control has been a dormant spray, oil or lime-sulphur, before growth starts in the spring. Parathion, malathion and cygon are now widely used and can be applied at any time of the year.

Fertilizing

Any fine animal or vegetable manure can be used for feeding bonsai. A vegetable manure such as cottonseed meal is all that is necessary for most trees. It can be administered in its regular granular form or as a liquid extract. The meal can be sprinkled over the soil about once every six weeks from midspring to midsummer. While you can be liberal in using it be sure not to be so liberal that it cakes. Flowering and fruit trees will need a supplement of bone meal.

Liquid commercial fertilizers such as Rapidgro and Hyponex may be used diluted according to manufacturer's directions. They can be applied with a watering can but do not sprinkle the foliage (only the soil). Do not over-fertilize. Liquid fertilizers should be used no more than three or four times a year. Start as the buds burst in the spring and continue until mid or late summer.

Repotting Bonsai

There are two reasons why it is necessary to repot dwarfed potted trees and change the soil and cut the roots. First, the root system gets pot-bound just as other potted plants and repotting improves drainage and soil aeration and provides new soil in which fine new roots can grow. The second reason is to encourage fine root growth by cutting back some of the larger roots and so keep the root system young.

The best time to repot is early in the spring just as bud growth starts. A second potting season occurs in late summer or early autumn. Pick a day that is overcast if you are working out-of-doors. Transplanting should be done in a place sheltered from drying winds. If repotting consists of shifting the plant to another container with only minor or no root-pruning it can be done anytime.

How often repotting is done depends on the growth rate of the tree. Evergreen conifers require repotting only once in three to five years, deciduous trees need it once every two or three years. If the tree is not pot-bound repotting can be delayed. If there is one to two inches of soil around the edge of the container that is not filled with roots it can be delayed for a year or two. A root-bound condition is present when roots have grown to a point where they are no longer able to gain sustenance from the soil. There will be roots growing close together around the outside of the ball.

Bonsai should not be watered just before repotting because it is difficult to remove the old soil if wet. New soil should also be dry so that it can be sifted and also can be readily placed around the roots.

Tools needed are one or more sieves for sifting soil, chopsticks for picking soil away and later for firming it, a trowel, shears, string, copper wire to use to tie trees into the container, a brush for scrubbing the container, a plastic screen or coconut fiber to cover drain holes in bottom of container, gravel to place in bottom over the wire, dried moss to place on top of soil, and a soil mixture suitable for the plant to be transplanted. The soil mixture generally should consist of loam, river sand, and well rotted leaf mold or manure—all completely dry. Mixtures and proportions vary with kinds of plants. Recommended proportions for pine trees are two parts loam, three parts river sand and one part leaf mold. Most other conifers require three parts loam, four parts river sand and one part leaf mold. Maples need three parts loam, one part river sand and two parts manure, and fruit and flowering trees need two parts loam and three parts manure. The ingredients should be sifted separately before measuring and then well mixed before using.

Procedure

1. Carefully take tree out of container and clean container with brush.
2. Prepare container for replacing the tree by running copper wire up through the holes of the container and positioning it for later tying the root ball into container. If the root ball is small string will be better than wire to tie tree into the container after it is root pruned. Cover the holes with screen or coconut fiber, cover the bottom with gravel, place enough of soil mixture over gravel to properly seat the tree ball after it is pruned and you are ready to proceed with work on the plant.
3. Untangle the roots from the root ball and using chopstick or pointed stick gently pick away soil from one-third the root mass on the sides and the lower half of the bottom of the ball being careful to remove the wire screening from the bottom. Be careful not to disrupt the soil around the trunk of the tree.
4. Using sharp shears trim roots taking one-third of fibrous mass on the sides and one-half of roots on the underside.
5. Position the tree back in the container which was prepared in step two. Place in center if container is round or square and one-third from end if rectangular or oval.
6. Work new soil around the roots by jabbing with chopstick. Do not press

with hand. Only chopsticks can make the soil work properly between the roots. Constantly add more soil mixture as you jab until no more is needed.

7. Fasten tree to container by pulling the wire up and twisting firmly. Insert strip of rubber between wire and root so wire will not cut the root.

8. Brush away excess soil and be sure soil is a fraction of an inch lower than sides of container so the water will not run off.

9. Spread a very thin dusting of soil over the surface and sprinkle dried powdered moss on top of the soil.

10. Now that the repotting operation is complete thoroughly saturate the newly planted bonsai by placing it in a tub of water in which the water level is nearly the same depth as the container. Also gently water from above.

Repotting with drastic root pruning is a shock to the tree and it will need special attention for a few weeks. Be sure to keep it in a shaded location protected from direct sun, wind and heavy rain. It is especially important that it be given extra water during this period. Never fertilize less than a month after repotting.

Training

The training of bonsai must continue all through the tree's life. Perfect shape can only be acquired and maintained by constant pruning and periodic wiring. Training begins when a plant is strong enough to stand treatment. In the case of a naturally dwarfed tree secured from the wilds it is better to wait until it is firmly established. In the case of a seedling, cutting or graft training will depend on rate of growth and health, but roughly speaking training can begin when the tree has formed shoots about two inches long.

Bonsai are classified in five main styles: formal upright, informal upright, slanting, semi-cascade, and cascade. No matter what style is chosen the three levels of heaven, man and earth are observed. This will be familiar to those who have studied Japanese flower arrangement. The three levels form a triangle with heaven, the top of the tree, as the apex and earth, the lowest level, forming the most acute angle. If the branch forming the earth angle is inadequate a rock or a small shrub can be placed near the roots for accent. When deciding on the style of a bonsai it is essential to study the tree carefully to determine what form will best suit its species and natural form. However, there are no rules of art on how to form a bonsai any more than there are on how to paint a picture. There are traditional forms and aesthetic considerations, schools of thought and standards followed.

In the two upright styles and the slanting style the lower branches are arranged in groups of three and start one-third the way up the trunk. About

51. *Growing on a stone slab is a Japanese white pine which is about forty years old.*

two-thirds of the total height of the tree should be revealed as trunk. Two branches are trained to come forward a little and the third extends out in back of the tree. The back branches are extremely important from the standpoint of shape and density of foliage. No one branch is immediately above the other because this would deprive the lower branch of water and sun. Branches are closer together near the top. In the formal upright style the top is erect. In the informal upright it bends slightly to the front. The trunk and branches of the slanting style should have an agreeable curve with the lowest branch spreading in the opposite direction to the slant and the top of the tree bending slightly forward.

The cascade styles start by growing upward from the soil. The full cascade turns downward very quickly and reaches below the level of the pot making it necessary to place it on a stand or on the edge of a table. The semi-cascade grows up for a distance and then cascades down at a less abrupt angle and may or may not reach the level of the bottom of the pot.

Wiring

Wiring is the most adaptable way of training branches and trunks of bonsai. It will take a little practice to become adept at it. Copper wire can be burned

119

in a fire and become flexible and still be durable. The Japanese use a rice-straw fire because the fire must not be too hot else the wire will become brittle and hard to coil. The wire should be removed from the fire as soon as it glows with a blue flame, cooled and used. Once annealed wire is bent it becomes hard again.

To apply the wire insert one end of it deep into the soil near the trunk to anchor it and then coil it upward around the trunk being cautious not to wrap it tight enough to injure the bark. The trunk is sometimes covered with rice straw or hemp bark before wraping the wire to prevent bark damage and sometimes the wire is covered with cloth or paper when used to train delicate soft-bark trees or shrubs. When the wire is in place the trunk is carefully bent. The branches are wrapped with wire and trained in the same manner. This technique is suitable for slender trunks and branches.

With stouter trunks bending must be done before wiring and the process is considerably more complicated.

Make frequent and careful checks to see that the wire is not cutting into the stem as it enlarges through growth. Remove carefully any binding wire as soon as discovered. You can rewire at a slightly different point if more bending is necessary. Wire can generally be removed after about a year's growth but it may take longer. Wiring and rewiring sometimes take several years before the tree attains the desired shape, especially if working with older trees.

The final beauty of the bonsai lies in its training and each person must decide for himself how the tree should be trained, whether it should be austerely classical in design or gracefully and informally cascading. Does this branch spoil the symmetry or should we add a rock to give more balance? Perhaps another pot should be chosen or the position of the plant in the container should be changed. We are working toward making a masterpiece!

Pruning and Nipping

The most important factor in keeping plants in bonsai proportion is pruning. Many species that make excellent bonsai would grow into huge trees if not constantly pruned and it is mainly by proper pruning that an artistic shape is achieved. No set of simplified rules concerning pruning and care is applicable to all the kinds of plants that can be grown as bonsai. The problem of describing methods that are simplified and concise is that the picture tends to become untrue because of the many exceptions and the many different ways of doing the same job.

The kind of pruning to control the size of bonsai limits the amount of new growth each year. It may be a once-a-year practice for some species or it may be a continuing process according to the growth habit of others. There is a common notion that pruning invigorates a plant and this is true when a plant is pruned *occasionally,* but pruning (aside from removing dead wood) is in actuality a dwarfing process if continued over a period of time. The amount of dwarfing is directly in proportion to the amount and frequency of pruning.

Top growth and root growth are interrelated and both root pruning (see repotting) and proper pruning of branches are important in dwarfing bonsai. The renewal of the root system is essential to the health of the trunk and branches and roots will remain healthy only if properly pruned.

In the case of deciduous trees such as maples pruning and nipping is done throughout the growing season. New growth is literally "nipped in the bud." Flowering trees and fruit trees are trimmed after they have flowered. Trees such as crepe myrtle and pomegranate which flower on new shoots may be trimmed in early spring to increase flowering but must then be left alone until after they bloom in the summer. Of course if an unsightly new shoot grows too long and spoils the shape of the tree it is cut off at any time. Junipers, cryptomeria and cypress are finger-nipped throughout the growing season as they are very prolific. The new growth (candles) on pine is snipped off in the spring with about five clusters of needles being allowed to remain on each candle. This will be enough to insure the health and vigor of the plant. Removal of all new seasonal growth would ultimately destroy the plant, but retention of part of it will encourage desirable compactness, multiplying of twig formation and thickening of trunk and branches. In the case of needle trees care must be taken not to cut through any part of the needles which are to remain.

When you visit Japan you may want to purchase a bonsai to enjoy in your room during your stay there, but please don't think of it in terms of something that costs only a few dollars and treat it as you would cut flowers to be enjoyed for a time and then thrown on the rubbish heap. This is shocking to the Japanese. Keep in mind that the bonsai you purchase may represent many years of love and care by some gardener whose father and grandfather may have tended it before him.

Our bonsai which we bought in Tokyo was left with other bonsai in the lovely garden of a small Japanese inn in Kyoto. I like to think of it there and long to return and see it again.

Obviously it would take volumes to thoroughly cover the subject of bonsai. I have barely touched the rudiments but I hope this brief chapter will tickle your curiosity, whet your appetite for more and cause you to pursue the subject further. I can't think of a more intriguing hobby for a person of any age. Time and patience and a little study are the requirements. One does not need a lot of space, elaborate equipment or a big outlay of money. Physical exertion can vary. You can confine it to a few minutes each day at fiddling jobs or you can expend tremendous energy on hikes and mountain-climbing expeditions in search of natural dwarfs. With luck and persistence you may find a natural dwarf that can be made into a really good bonsai in a short time. It is possible that such a bonsai after a year's training may look older and more finished than others that have been in training for years!

The amateur should not be discouraged by the talk of heavy responsibility and the many years spent in training and caring for a prize specimen. Absolute perfection is extremely rare and enjoyment does not depend on it. Also there are short cuts by which handsome bonsai can be created in months instead of years. Anyone who is accustomed to a garden will find from a little study that the technique of growing bonsai is largely an adaptation of what he already knows. The care demanded by bonsai is not necessarily more mysterious than that required by many of our ordinary potted plants.

Although the care and patience that go into this cherished art of Japan is infinite, please remember that while to a connoisseur only a fully trained ancient tree is worthy of note, to an amateur grower the bonsai tree is both beautiful and exciting from its very first stages and many bonsai of real beauty have been trained for only one to three years.

IKEBANA

V

The art of arranging flowers known as *ikebana* or "living flowers" is an aesthetic achievement peculiar to Japan. *Ikebana,* like the art of gardening, aims by means of trees and plants to represent life in nature as it centers around human life. By retaining a suggestion of the natural growth of flowers and of the landscape to which they belong the Japanese have developed ways of arranging flowers that enables man to grasp nature at her loveliest and to elevate his mind to spiritual beauty. The floral art of Japan is based on aesthetic rules derived from a profound knowledge of plant life gained by close and constant observation. The spirit of Japanese flower arrangement is to make a thing of beauty out of commonplace material. No flower or shrub is too humble to use.

The heart of the Japanese people is much affected by the natural beauty around them. Their way of looking at beautiful things is deeply influenced by the natural changes that take place. They are not only sensitive to the beauty of the moment but ardently admire the movement of beauty. Thus, the changes in nature have been closely related to the changes in the human heart. Human beings as well as flowers and plants are products of nature and subject to natural changes. Therefore, according to the Japanese way of thinking man must grow and progress in perfect harmony with nature. They treat nature as respectfully as they treat their fellow men and are moved by its beauty just as they are moved by beautiful deeds of men. Nature seems to the Japanese to enwrap all living creatures in her beauty and love and have a healing and comforting effect upon the heart which turns to her with love and sincerity.

A floral arrangement in Japan is a sincere attempt to bring a small part of nature into the house as an expression of nature's grandeur and power. The term "flower arrangement" is used in a rather broad sense. To people acquainted with only Western flower arrangement the word flower suggests blossoms with or without a certain amount of stems and foliage and other material that is necessary to make an attractive bouquet. In Japan the word *hana,* the closest English equivalent to flower, refers not only to the blossom but also to the stem and branches of flowering plants and trees and to the branches of flowerless trees and plants. In fact the branches of certain evergreens and other flowerless trees and plants such as pine, maple and bamboo are given the highest rank among *hana.* Thus blossoms are regarded as only one detail of the composition and possess little artistic value if separated from those lines of growth that give it its character.

Priests, poets, philosophers and aesthetics through the centuries have cherished and developed the art of arranging flowers and it exercises a strong influence on the lives of all Japanese. However, the popularity of *ikebana* is not limited to Japan—it has spread all over the world.

History

There are conflicting records concerning the origin of the art of arranging flowers but it is always attributed to Buddhism which was introduced into Japan around the middle of the sixth century. Although it came to Japan from China along with other forms of art the practice of arranging flowers as it developed in Japan is without prototype and is a purely Japanese cultural achievement.

Ikenobo was the first school of flower arrangement in Japan and has an authentic age of thirteen hundred years. It is the parent to all the hundreds of schools that have come after. Ono-no Imoko, a member of the Imperial Court, is regarded as the founder of this school. His sponsor, Prince Shotoku Taishi, regent to the Empress Suiko, was a fervent Buddhist under whose leadership Japanese civilization made outstanding progress. It was he who recognized the moral and intellectual benefits of the religion and built numerous temples that became seats of learning.

In 607 Ono-no Imoko was sent to China as the first official Japanese ambassador. China was then at the apex of her political and artistic development and Ono-no Imoko along with priests, artists, scholars, and craftsmen who were also chosen to study abroad absorbed China's cultural and religious wealth. They gained a knowledge of offering flowers in the temples and of designing gardens with bridges and ponds and other features which until that time were unknown in Japan. After the death of his patron, Prince Shotoku, in 627 Ono-no Imoko took the priestly tonsure and retired to a small priests' lodge with a lovely garden and lake which Shotoku Taishi had planned from Chinese models. The lodge was situated behind the main hall of Rokkakudo, a small six-sided Buddhist temple at Kyoto, founded by Shotoku in 587. There, according to tradition,

Ono-no Imoko devoted the remainder of his days to meditation and prayer and arranging flowers as offerings to Buddha. He taught that a flower arrangement was a natural expression of the unity of all life and a floral offering for the altar should symbolize and express the part that the love of flowers plays in harmonizing man's soul and nature. Within his lifetime Ono-no Imoko's method of arranging flowers became famous and priests from other temples came to learn his way. Such arrangements were said to be in the style of the floral offerings at the "hermitage by the lake" or Ikenobo. Thus was founded the first known school of flower arranging. Ikenobo school is still in existence and one of the most prominent.

Ono-no Imoko had assumed the name Sen-mu during his guardianship of Rokkakudo and thereafter those who succeeded him as high priest of the temple and head of Ikenobo adopted a name with a prefix Sen. At present Ikenobo Sen-ei, a forty-fifth generation descendant in direct line from the first Ikenobo headmaster, is the chief priest of the Rokkakudo Temple and devotes himself to preserving the heritage left by his great forefathers. The *rikka* arrangements in Plates 52 and 53 were designed by Mr. Ikenobo.

Some of my most cherished memories relate to the time I have spent at Rokkakudo Temple studying in the very cradle of flower arranging.

History of Rikka Style

Floral compositions which developed under the influence of Buddhism were at first restricted to religious purposes. Later they were also used for secular decoration at the Imperial Court. The most ancient systematized style of these arrangements was a formal composition known as *rikka* or *rikkwa* meaning "standing-up plant cuttings." These arrangements commonly ranged in height from four to six feet but were often much larger. It is from the *rikka* form that all present-day simplified flower arrangement styles are descended.

The *rikka* arrangement has enjoyed an unprecedented period of popularity. The first known treatise giving definite rules and nomenclature to the different members of a *rikka* arrangement was written by Sen-kei Ikenobo in the fifteenth century. Through his teaching and that of the Masters who followed him *rikka* arrangements were brought to a high degree of excellence. Sen-O Ikenobo did much to perfect this style during the sixteenth century and Ikenobo Sen-ko, the thirty-second head of Ikenobo School, brought *rikka* to final perfection and crystalized the rules that are still observed today. This was during the seventeenth century which was the Golden Age of the *rikka* form when elaborate exhibitions were held at the Imperial Palace, in temples, and at the homes of feudal lords. During this period *rikka* arrangements grew larger and larger to match the splendor and magnificence of the huge mansions and temples where they were displayed. They were extremely popular down to the middle of the nineteenth century. By 1765 peace had been restored and the lives of the people stabilized permitting the general public to accumulate enough wealth to enjoy the niceties of life. In keeping with the change of times *ikebana* underwent modifications of style to accommodate the change of setting from large mansions to small houses. Finally when *rikka* did not always meet the day's demand for beauty with its fixed forms and exacting use of materials a new form of *ikebana* emerged known as *shoka*.

History of Shoka

The new and simplified *shoka* style which appeared at the beginning of the eighteenth century offered limitless possibilities for variation and as it spread to the general public many masters broke with Ikenobo School in Kyoto, which had enjoyed a virtual monopoly in the area of flower arrangement for centuries, and established schools and styles of their own. By the nineteenth century *shoka* form had supplanted *rikka* in popularity. All the new schools based their styles on the asymmetrical form of three branches but used new angles of branch placement and used new terminology. Popular at this time was the term *seika* used instead of the term *shoka* which was favored by Ikenobo School.

History of Nageire

Nageire arrangements were developed in the sixteenth century and their simplicity contrasted sharply with the gorgeous style of *rikka* that was also popular at the same time. The two styles reflect the contrasting aspects of the culture of the day. The warrior class had taken over the rule of the land and ostentatious pomp and splendor characterized their culture. On the other hand, however, there developed the entirely opposite tendency in art which now characterizes the uniquely Japanese elegant simplicity and quiet taste expressed by the subtle terms *wabi* and *sabi*. Continuous upheavel in the country made the people, influenced by Buddhist thinking, despair of this transient world. So it is not surprising that the gorgeous style of *rikka* and the simple *nageire* styles flourished at the same time.

The ideas of naturalness and simplicity, frugality and restraint found in Zen teachings were mirrored in these later styles of flower arrangement which adopted to some extent the *rikka* but in a simplified form. *Nageire* was used to add its subtle touch to the tea room. Under the influence of frugality and rustic simplicity that governed the tea room a flower composition often took the form of a simple arrangement of a single flower and its leaves or a spray of a flowering shrub. The most famous master of this type of arrangement was Sen-no Rikyu who also perfected the tea cult.

Sen-no Rikyu and the great General Hideyoshi for whom Rikyu often arranged flowers (even on the battlefield) are credited with popularizing the *nageire* style. Rikyu averred that the art of *nageire* was essentially spiritual and left no book or writing on the subject, believing that words were inadequate to communicate the true meaning of the art. In notes left by one of Rikyu's disciples he is credited with saying that the worst of all sins in all arrangements is to make a show of one's work. "The best thing," he declared, "is the unforced or natural." He cautioned against overdoing decoration and artificiality. "The deeper one penetrates into understanding nature," he stated, "the more conscious will he become that natural beauty far surpasses the artificial and he will appreciate the simple and unadorned beauty more than anything else." These words of Rikyu are significant in the appreciation of *nageire*, the simple and natural arrangement.

It is intriguing to realize that this tragic man, who was born in an age of civil wars and knew bloodshed and slaughter all his life, hated artificiality believing it to be the source of all evil. He insisted on naturalness which he stated was the fount of life and beauty in all things especially in the art of flower arrangement. It seems that men born in a peaceful age seek beauty in artificiality while those born in the age of war and turmoil find beauty and true joy in the simple and natural. How interesting it is to realize that a man's attitude towards flowers reflect the age in which he is born!

History of Moribana

Moribana-form arrangement was developed at the turn of the century and owes its being to Western influence. As Western-style furnishings and Western-style rooms came along a change also took place in flower arrangement. Although similar arrangements had existed since olden times it was not until the period between 1868-1912 that the style became fixed. The famous Ohara School of flower arrangement was founded by the originator of *moribana* as we know it today. The composition of *moribana* was founded on *shoka's* three line principle of *shin, soe* and *tai*. It is the most widely used style today in both Japanese and Western homes.

One might imagine that flower arrangement is merely a traditional art of Japan the forms of which were fixed centuries ago but the fact is that the forms changed from age to age and are still changing. The future undoubtedly will hold many more changes. Unlike its sister arts *cha-no-yu* (tea ceremony) and *Noh* drama, which have undergone very few changes since the rules governing them were fixed nearly four hundred years ago, the art of flower arranging has been subject to many vicissitudes in history. Both *cha-no-yu* and *Noh* drama have existed apart from the actual life of the people but the art of flower arrangement has had a vital connection with daily life. In other words *cha-no-yu* has had the tea house and the *Noh* drama has had its own stage, but flower arrangement has existed in the homes of the people and become a necessary part of their daily life. Both flower arranging and painting have changed as the lives of the Japanese people changed.

Ikebana Today

Arrangements done in Japanese homes nowadays are usually in either the *nageire* or *moribana* styles or free style. This is due to the extremely crowded conditions of urban life. In rural areas the classical style is still the most popular. In many homes the use of flowers is restricted to the small household shrines. On Shinto shrines small branches of the sacred *sakaki* tree are placed on the *kamidana,* god-shelf. Buddhist home altars employ mixed bouquets as decoration. These are known as *kubana* meaning "offering flowers." This type of arrangement is used also at large weddings. I attended a very stylish hotel wedding in Japan. The Shinto altar in the ceremony room held a small arrangement of *sakaki.* The tables in the banquet hall were decorated with large mixed bouquets of flowers which were used with wide runners of red satin ribbon on white cloths. The colors of the flowers were also mixed but red and white predominated, red and white being the male and female colors symbolizing health and happiness.

Many large flower shows are held each year in Japan where the exhibitors do their utmost to create outstanding arrangements. The exhibitors are usually masters and teachers of various schools. These exhibitions are seldom competitive however. The space allotted to each exhibitor is large, usually varying in width from three to nine feet. These large arrangements provide considerable scope to the exhibitors for demonstrating their creativity.

Some of the most interesting and publicized work is intended for public display alone and is not suitable for the *tokonoma* or the family living room. Some of the most famous works of Japanese masters are interesting mostly for their shock quality. This parallels many of the classes in our own flower shows. This type of arrangement offers only limited helpfulness to a novice arranger hoping to learn.

Since 1945 with the termination of World War II and the influx of Occidental aesthetic standards there has been a movement to extend the scope of flower arrangement to include objects such as iron, brass, stone, feathers, glass, plaster and plastic. This movement known as the avant-garde movement has swept through the traditional world of Japan's floral art and tradition often giving way to free-form expression and individualism. Whereas before the plant in its natural state was used in *ikebana* now plants are often twisted, painted and even burnt to meet the requirements of abstract art. In leading *ikebana* shows flowers are often combined with non-organic matter and sometimes "flower arrangements" are made entirely of non-organic matter! Regardless of its merits and demerits the avant-garde movement is sure to affect the future trends. The world has always changed and young people have always wanted "new and modern" things. They have always rebelled against custom. In the twentieth century the pace has been accelerated and the results make one a bit dizzy. It seems that the senses of contemporary people require strong stimuli to provoke emotion. Complaints of the effect of Western culture on the Far East have been myriad and mostly justified. Tokyo, Osaka, and Kobe are great modern Westernized cities on the surface, but if the traveler will go just a little off the main lines he will move out of the hectic twentieth century into the nineteenth and even further back.

The Japanese have been gobbling up Western "civilization" for a century now and sometimes one has the feeling that the ravages of "progress" have invaded and at times destroyed the charm of classical Japan. A consoling thought —the Japanese have gobbled up and digested other civilizations before this and then turned back enough to retain much of their old culture and charm entwined with the new.

So it is with *ikebana*. While the avant-garde movement dominates the flower arrangement scene its principles are founded in traditional *ikebana*. Modern trends are exciting and should be explored. Owing to the influence of the avant-garde movement all the older schools including the traditional Ikenobo, Enshu-ryu, and Ko-ryu schools teach free-form arrangements as well as the classics.

Never before in history has Japanese flower arrangement enjoyed greater popularity than it does today. Many hundreds of different schools have millions of teachers and students. It has been estimated that there are between two and three thousand schools.

Even though today's trends are strongly avant-grade, we should make a study of the traditional styles of *ikebana* to gain a firm artistic foundation regardless of the course of history.

Students of art in any of its forms, be it painting, sculpture, music or literature, discover the existence of a certain definite, universal and eternal form into which his effort must be fitted to have enduring quality. The painter must in his two-dimensional field learn the intelligent handling of proportion, contrast and texture. The sculptor with his three dimensions, the musician with his mystic use of the laws of audio harmony, and the writer building structures of words are all artists faced with the problems of form. The flower arranger and the landscape designer, using chiefly living forms, are confronted with the same kind of problems and more. Consideration must be given the judicious use of proportion, balance, third-dimensional values, color relationships, unity of design, suitability and on and on. To add to the complexities there is an iron-clad rule that says "the master bends form to his will while the uninspired are literally governed by it." In other words the master knows what he can do and is in truth the master. He knows when and how to break established rules.

The Japanese artist creates a special kind of beauty that includes patina and tradition of age, incompleteness and irregularity of design, suggestiveness, and calmness of spirit that comes from lack of artifice, a philosophy that pervades Japanese art and conduct.

To Summarize:

Five distinct styles of *ikebana* have evolved over the past five hundred years as follows:

1. Rikka, fifteenth century.
2. Shoka (Seika) eighteenth century.
Note: *Rikka* and *shoka* are both classical styles.
3. Nageire, sixteenth century.
Note: Although *nageire* was developed before *shoka* it is usually classed with *moribana* due to the fact that as it is practiced today it evolved along with *moribana*.
4. Moribana, 1900.
5. Modern, 1930.

Under modern we will discuss free-style, abstract, and avant-garde. Now let us take another look at the five styles.

CLASSICAL FORMS OF IKEBANA: RIKKA

Unfortunately very little has been written on the *rikka* style in recent times, yet this is a living art in Japan today and its spirit pervades other newer forms of flower arrangement. *Rikka* arrangements are seen at the large all-Japan exhibits. Ikenobo school is teaching a charming modified form known as salon *rikka* which is lovely in any type of room where a mass arrangement is desired. In this contemporary *rikka* form classical models provide the basis upon which the arranger improvises according to his inspiration using modern techniques, and designing sizes to fit his needs. *Rikka* style occupies a permanent place in modern Japanese arrangement and I believe it will become more and more popular with Western arrangers as they learn more about it.

Most present writings on Japanese floral art simply state that *Rikka* arrangement is the most ancient systematized form and then dismiss it as belonging to a more leisurely and opulent period of history and as being too complex, time-consuming, and too large for modern taste. It is true that *rikka* style is difficult and time-consuming to learn and requires serious study before the arranger achieves satisfactory results, but as a studied form of floral art *rikka* is supreme. It is practical both for its aesthetic appeal and for the technical proficiency which it develops in the arranger. This proficiency can be transplanted to other forms of arrangement. For the serious student of ikebana *rikka* is an exhilarating experience.

52. *Classical* rikka *arrangement in a traditional bronze container by Mr. Sen-ei Ikenobo XLV, head of the Ikenobo School at Rokkaku-do Temple. The materials are pine, pampas grass, loquat, camellia, hiba, sorbus, wax tree, beech tree, and pinks.*

While *rikka* constitutes a vast field of study and it would be impossible for us to pursue a really exhaustive study of this style, a study of the fundamental principles will give insight into the origins of Japanese flower arrangement, enhance the understanding of the art, and develop technical skill in all forms of arrangement. At the same time you will be creating outstanding mass arrangements. Here I shall discuss only the making of contemporary *rikka* arrangements with a hope that it will serve as a stimulus to those who are anxious to gain an insight into this fascinating style of arranging flowers.

131

Nine Principal Branches with English Meaning:

Shin—True, straight branch
Soe—Supporting branch
Uke—Receiving branch
Sho-shin—Perfectly straight branch (real center)
Mikoshi—Overhanging branch
Nagashi—Flowering branch
Hikae—Waiting or reserve branch
Do—Body or trunk of the arrangement
Mae-oki—Anterior branch

Other Branches:

Ushiro-gakoi—Branches which finish arrangement in the back.
Ki-dome—Last grass or flower material to be added
Ashirai—Any supporting branch

Lengths of Branches

Once the height of the main branch, *shin,* is determined all the other branches conform to it according to established proportions. The height of *shin* ranges from about three to five times the height of the container. *Soe* is roughly two thirds of *shin,* and *nagashi* extends out the same distance from the arrangement's median axis as *soe.* As a general rule no branches protrude beyond the scalene triangle formed by the tips of these three branches. *Uke* and *hikae* should be eqdidistant from the arrangement's median axis, *mikoshi* and the supporting *shin* branch should be the same height and the top of *sho-shin* should rise slightly above the level of *soe.* If *shin, soe* and *nagashi* are removed the arrangement would still be in perfect balance. Likewise it would still be in balance if *mikoshi, uke* and *hikae* are removed.

Mae-oki extends to the lower front. From its tip through to the back of the arrangement there should be a depth that is almost the width of the arrangement.

Placement of Lines

Shin is placed first slightly behind center of container followed by *sho-shin* in front of *shin* and in the true center. *Do* and *mae-oki* follow. All three are in front of *shin.* All other lines are placed to the sides and back of these.

In very large traditional *rikka* construction mechanics for holding the lines in place were made by tying straw very tightly in bundles and cutting lengths which when fully inserted in the container were about two inches below the rim of the container. These lengths were then tied firmly together to make a bundle thick enough to fit very tightly in the container. The stems of plant

53. *(Left) A contemporary* rikka *arrangement in a pottery container designed by Mr. Sen-ei Ikenobo XLV contains pampas grass, larkspur, lily, loquat leaves, chrysanthemums, fern, sorbus, mountain ash, and box-tree.*

54. *(Right) A contemporary* rikka *arrangement using modern technique, in a simple pottery container. Materials are pine, gladiolus, aspidistra, camellia foliage, pandanus, roses, anemones, baby's breath, and azalea.*

material were placed directly into the straw. Special funnel shaped tubes of bamboo or metal were sometimes made to hold grass material and weak-stemmed flowers. These were tied onto strong stems or length of wood which were placed into the straw base. For today's smaller contemporary forms of *rikka* the mechanics are much simpler. An easy technique which was taught me at Rokkaudo Temple was this: Fill the container with gravel or small pebbles to within

133

about three inches of the top of container. On top of this place a good heavy needlepoint holder with a piece of wet paper between the holder and gravel to keep it from slipping. The needlepoint holder can be hidden by more pebbles or by moss when the arrangement has been completed. I find orchid tubes fastened to sticks invaluable in placing short stemmed flowers, grasses and other weak stems in the design.

The time spent in mastering the rules and techniques governing the construction of *rikka* arrangements will more than repay you in acquiring confidence and speed in making more informal arrangements. The basic principles are art principles and any arrangement of flowers from a single bloom with its leaves to a large church decoration will be more quickly done and give more aesthetic pleasure if these principles are followed.

55. *(Left) Shoka arrangement using only two gladiolus stems and foliage. The classical container is known as* shiun *(purple cloud) and is placed on a* usuban.

56. *(Right) A shoka arrangement showing the exaggeration of line that is typical of some schools.*

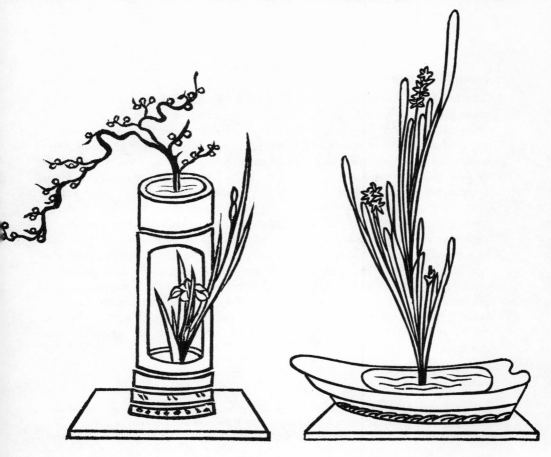

57. (Left) Bamboo, a popular garden plant and a much-used building material, is also made into flower containers of many styles. This one has two tiers and is used for double shoka arrangements. One is of iris and the other of flowering branches.

58. (Right) There are three classical boat arrangements, each depicting a stage in the voyage: incoming, outgoing, and in port. This old print shows narcissus arranged to symbolize a boat in port.

SHOKA

As mentioned in the history of *ikebana* the *shoka* form developed from the *rikka* and is an abbreviation and simplification of it. Like all other styles of *ikebana*, regardless of period and school, it is an asymmetrical form built on the principal branches of unequal lengths. The longest branch is called *shin* (primary branch) the branch of intermediate height is known as *soe* (secondary branch), and the shortest of the three is called *tai* (supplementary branch). They are also known respectively: *ten* (heaven), *jin* (man), and *chi* (earth).

135

Length of Stems

The height of *shin* above the water level may be from one and a half to three times the height or width of the container depending on the container, type of plant material, and placement of the completed arrangement. *Soe* should be two thirds of the height of *shin,* and *tai* one third the height of *shin.* These measurements give the arrangement three levels: the upper level which comprises the *shin* or *shin* group of branches; the middle level which comprises the *soe* or *soe* group of branches; and the lower level which is made up of the *tai* or *tai* group of branches. A *shoka* arrangement may be made up of three branches or many. Each group may contain only one branch or many. However, for best results each group will be made with three levels similar to *shin, soe,* and *tai.* The number of branches or flowers necessary depends on the plant material used. An odd number of branches is used in each group as well as in the arrangement as a whole. Proportion is an essential requirement in any flower arrangement. Cut the branch in the rear of the main branch first. It will be longer than the branch in front of the main branch. Generally speaking, always make the branch in the rear of any group's main branch longer than the one in front of the main branch.

59. *A traditional hanging bamboo boat was used for this arrangement designed by the author while studying at Rokkaku-do Temple in Kyoto. The placement of lines depicts an outgoing boat. The long trailing branch symbolizes an oar and is used in addition to the regular* shin, soe, *and* tai. *By making this a left-hand instead of a right-hand arrangement an incoming boat would be represented.*

60. (Left) Often tree materials or leaves are used for shin and soe lines and tai is formed by a nejime of flowers.

61. (Right) Three branches of mahonia form a long-lasting shoka arrangement in a classical container.

Whereas the *shin* group and the *soe* group both decrease regularly, when the *tai* group consists of more than two branches it forms a "valley" and calls for special attention. The branch within the *tai* group which is nearest to *shin* is termed *tai-shin* (in other words the *shin* branch of the *tai* group), and though the *tai* branch is usually one third the height of *shin*, the *tai-shin* may be as much as half the height of *shin*.

137

Hongatte and Gyakugatte (Higatte)

The *shin* branch of a *shoka* arrangement is curved. It should curve to the left rear or to the right rear depending on whether the arrangement is a *gyakugatte,* left-hand, or a *hongatte,* right-hand, one. The maximum curvature should fall within the second fifth from the bottom if the branch were divided into five equal parts. The top of *shin* should be in line with its base and the expansion of its curve should not go beyond the outer edge of the container.

The position of *soe* is determined by the curvature of *shin*. If *shin* curves to the left rear the *soe* is placed to the left rear of *shin*. If *shin* curves to the right rear *soe* is placed to the right rear of *shin*. The *tai* is placed to the right front or to the left front in line with *soe*. If an imaginary line is drawn from *tai* through *shin* to *soe* it would be perfectly straight and lie at about a forty-five degree angle from the left-to-right axis of the arrangement and oblique to the viewer.

Plant material is held firmly in the container by means of a *kubari* or forked stick inserted in the mouth of the container with the apex of the triangle toward the arranger. All stems are placed within the fork and wedged firmly in the crotch of the *kubari* with another stick called a *komi*. When finished a *shoka* arrangement must emerge from the container like a single stem. The stem must be free of leaves or flowers for a height of three to four inches above the container's mouth. This is known as the *mizugiwa* or "water's edge." *Shoka* arrangements are usually displayed on a plain or scrolled base or low table except in the case of those made in baskets. *Shoka* arrangements are also very effective when done in shallow contemporary containers in which case the *kubari* can be inserted into a metal ring which may or may not have a needle-point holder under it. Rocks or pebbles are then used to conceal the *kubari*.

Although *shoka* arrangements are governed by definite rules and set patterns they offer the arranger tremendous opportunity to create outstandingly beautiful and diversified designs which can be achieved through choice of plant materials, containers and bases. This style of arrangement is lovely in any type of home.

It is a well known and accepted fact that a classical Japanese flower arrangement surpasses in beauty and depth of meaning any other method of grouping flowers.

NAGEIRE

The *nageire* form is an unstudied, natural arrangement of plant material in a tall container. It does not prescribe rigid rules as do *rikka* and *shoka* styles but leaves more room for variation according to the nature of the material used. The word *nageire* means "to throw in," giving the impression that the plant

62. (Left) The arrangement on the left is a right-hand (hongatte) arrangement. The one on the right is a left-hand (gyakugatte or higatte) arrangement. You can clearly see how the plant material fits into the kubari in the arrangement at the right.

63. (Right) A pottery vase holds an arrangement for the New Year designed by Mr. Choca Adachi, headmaster of the Adachi School. Symbolic materials —camellia, pine, and plum—were used.

material is simply or carelessly tossed into the container. This is far from the truth. Each branch, each flower, and each container presents an individual problem and requires different handling. Usually when the main branches are securely anchored, the others can be easily balanced in the design. *Nageire* arrangements are classified into three groups: upright, incline, and cascade or flowing. There are many variations to the basic patterns, one school listing thirty. This offers infinite possibilities and patterns to follow.

The natural looking, seemingly casual effect of the *nageire* style appeals to modern taste. One of the principal characteristics of this type of arrangement

 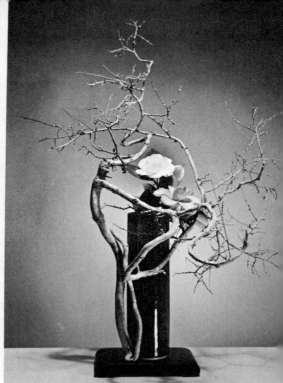

64. *(Left) Since ancient times baskets have been a favorite container for flower arrangement. Bamboo and two roses were used to create a charming* nageire *design. The bases of lacquer and bamboo balance the slanting design. (Arranged by Mrs. W. B. Garrison.)*

65. *(Right) In this free-style* nageire *arrangement a gray branch is placed outside a blue pottery container which holds pink camellias.*

lies in the small quantity of plant material used. Often the arrangement consists of no more than one well-shaped branch and a few sprays of flowers at its base.

MORIBANA

Moribana, meaning "piled up flowers," is the style most often seen in Japan today. It is also the style most appreciated by Occidentals and very easy to learn. The impact of the West has been felt in Japan for a century now and the *moribana* style of arranging flowers was developed to meet the need for an arrangement to be used outside the tokonoma and viewed from more than one side. This informal style is constructed in a low, flat container and the plant material is inserted in a needlepoint holder. This style is the easiest of all to learn and with a little practice all the basic patterns can be created. There are a number of variations to the basic patterns which gives wide scope to the arranger.

Nageire and *moribana,* like *shoka,* are based on three main lines which represent the three great parts of the universe—heaven, man, and earth. Heaven is dominant, man is second and earth is last. There may be lines to strengthen the three main lines, but the assisting lines must not be any longer or more dominant than the line they assist. These lines, or groups of lines, have definite

66. (Left) One branch of clipped pine and one cone in a modern black pottery container form a long-lasting moribana *arrangement. The base is black lacquer edged in red.*

67. (Right) *Iris is one of the most popular flowers in Japanese flower arrangement. Here it is used in a multi-placement* moribana *design. The needlepoint holders are concealed with water-tumbled stones from a mountain stream.*

68. *Branches of white cercis and daffodils in a green ceramic* suiban *form a pleasant* moribana *arrangement for spring.*

relationship to each other. The length of the main heaven stem or line sets the scale for the whole arrangement. Its length depends on the size of the container, the space where the arrangement is to be placed, and type of material. All other lines are in proportion to this main line and grouped about it. Stem lengths vary according to styles and schools. Generally, heaven is one and one half to five times the width of a flat container or height of a tall one. Man is two thirds to three fourths of heaven, and earth is usually one third of heaven, or one half to three fourths of man.

Mastering Japanese arrangement is a life's work. However, the person who has neither the time nor inclination to delve into the subject may well concentrate on the technique of making even one of the basic forms, using it as a pattern for creating a wide variety of lovely arrangements.

The study of Japanese flower arrangement will develop a sensitivenss to line, proportion, balance, and rhythm. Memorize the proportions of plant material to the container, the proportions and direction of the lines of the three main groups and use this knowledge to create flower arrangements of beauty, distinction and originality.

69. (Left) Cope branches and pink roses were used to fashion this basic *upright* moribana *design. The container is a gray iron boat.*

70. (Right) Mahonia with yellow tulips in a bronze container form an *upright* moribana *arrangement.*

THE THREE STYLES OF CLASSICAL ARRANGEMENT

Classical arrangements whether of the *rikka* or *shoka* form may be done in one of three styles; *shin, gyo* and *so*. They are interpreted as formal, semi-formal and informal respectively. Actually any arrangement done in one of the three styles is a formal arrangement. In using English equivalents the student is often confused and has difficulty trying to assimilate the meaning. I will attempt to explain.

When applied to styles of flower arrangement the word *shin* literally means "true" and expresses straightness or perpendicularity. *Gyo* means "moving" and

71. *(Left)* Shin *style* rikka *arrangement: 1.* Shin 2. Sho-shin 3. Mikoshi 4. Soe 5. Do 6. Hikae 7. Mae-oki 8. Nagashi 9. Uke.

72. *(Right)* Gyo *style of* rikka *arrangement with nine principal branches:* 1. Shin 2. Sho-shin 3. Soe 4. Uke 5. Do 6. Hikae 7. Mae-oki 8. Nagashi 9. Mikoshi.

connotes moderate linear movement. The word *so* means "grass" (bending in the wind) and connotes forceful linear movement.

In the *rikka* form *shin* is characterized by a straight primary branch, the *gyo* by a somewhat curved primary branch and the *so* style is typically a low, broad arrangement done in a shallow container filled with sand. See drawings 71, 72 and 73.

In the *shoka* form the *shin* style is characterized by a primary branch which has a slight right or left curvature. Arrangements of this style must always be made in a slender narrow-mouth container such as a bamboo cylinder. In the *gyo* style the curvature of the primary branch is accentuated. This type calls for a wide-mouth container such as an *usubata* or basket. The *so* style is characterized by sweeping, free-flowing lines and is suited to low, shallow containers and to hanging arrangements. See drawings 74 and 75.

In and Yo, Yin and Yang

In classical Japanese flower arrangement students are confronted with two mysterious terms called *in* and *yo*. The Orientals are always aware of cosmic forces and Oriental art is characterized as a whole in its component parts by the negative and positive forces of *in* and *yo*. These are Japanese terms for the two Chinese characters of *Yin* and *Yang*. The phenomenal world is viewed as pervaded by these two contrary yet complementary energies. Both forces are always present. Unequal and incomplete in themselves, together they provide a perfect balance of inequality and make possible the existence of all things. Order reigns in the cosmos as long as the positive is in proportion with the negative and disorder comes when there is a predominance of one over the other. Ideally there is a perfect balance between the two.

In and *yo* are used to express many other paired associations such as follows in the *in* and *yo* or negative and positive order: darkness and light; passive and active; weak and strong; evil and good; left and right; earth and heaven; moon and sun; material and spiritual; forever opposed, forever united.

Examination of almost any form of plant life will show that it grows upward out of the earth *(in)* toward heaven *(yo)*. The part of the plant that faces the sun *(yo)* is the front or positive side and the part facing the dark earth *(in)* is its back or negative side. The careful discrimination and balancing of the positive and negative surfaces of plant material is one of the fundamental secrets of successful flower arrangement.

It was by applying the concept of *in* and *yo*, already in use in other fields of art, to the *rikka* arrangements that flower masters achieved their ideal and *rikka* became an established art that served as a fountainhead of all later styles of flower arrangement.

Example of In and Yo in Ikebana

How *in* and *yo* apply to flower arrangement can easily be seen in the *shoka* form. The *shin* or primary branch ordinarily has a natural curve owing to its tendency during growth to bend to the sun. The orientation of the *shin* branch in the container determines the position of the *soe* or secondary branch. The direction in which the *shin* curves defines its *yo* (positive) side and the *soe* must be placed accordingly. If the *shin* branch curves to the viewer's left the *soe* branch will be placed to its left with the *yo* side of *shin* facing the *yo* side of *soe*. In this case the completed design is called a right-hand arrangement. Conversely, if the *soe* branch stands to the right of the *shin* branch the arrangement is a left-hand one. An exception to the rule is when the *soe* and *tai* are reversed, the *soe* thus standing on the *in* side of *shin* and *tai* on its *yo* side. In such a case the *soe* is known as "inverted *soe*." In the normal *shoka* arrangement the *tai* branch is so placed in the container that if any imaginary line is drawn from the tip of *soe* through *shin* to the tip of *tai* it would be straight and the *yo* side of *tai* must face the *in* side of *shin*. Due to the fact that the three branches are in a line and their axes placed at a forty-five degree angle to the viewer the arrangement has a balance and completeness which would otherwise be lacking. See drawing 76.

The application of the principles of *in* and *yo* to *ikebana* abolishes symmetry and prevents monotony. Light and dark colors, left and right curves, buds and full-blown flowers, front and back of leaves, short and long stems are all principles of *in* and *yo* and contribute balance and contrast and heighten the effect of a flower arrangement. The aim of a traditional flower arrangement is to express a moment of arrested growth in the life of a living plant. It is by applying the principles of *in* and *yo* that this can be achieved.

73. So *style* rikka *arrangement.*

74. *(Left)* Shin *style* shoka. *Only three leaves were used to create this lovely, understated* shoka *arrangement, but it would grace any setting and remain fresh for weeks.*

75. *(Center)* Gyo *style* shoka. *A* usubata *holds a complicated* shoka *arrangement of seventeen aspidistra leaves and flowers. Fewer leaves can be used to make a beautiful, long-lasting arrangement and the flowers can be replaced as they fade.*

76. *(Right) The drawing shows clearly the curve of the main branch as it turns to the sun.*

MODERN IKEBANA

Flower arranging has come a long, long way since the days when the priests first placed flowers at the altar in tribute to Buddha.

The study of Japanese flower arrangement today can be divided into three phases. The first and very important phase is the study of the classical styles and the basic patterns of *moribana* and *nageire*. In this phase fresh flowers and plants are used in traditional containers. This form of arrangement is suited to

77. (Left) *Bulrush, bamboo, equisetum, box and chrysanthemums in a rough brown pottery container. Though the arrangement is modern, it is based on an established* moribana *pattern.*

78. (Right) *Calathea, heliconia, and a monsteria leaf were used in designing the modern upright* moribana *arrangement. The container is of black pottery.*

79. (Opposite, left) *A twisted limb of long-leaf pine forms the dominant line of this free-style arrangement. A wisteria branch, camellia foliage and tulips complete it.*

80. (Opposite, right) *Branches of sparkleberry frame the bold, modern container which holds two lilies in a free-style arrangement.*

any type of home, office, or background. Many people are content with the natural beauty of plant life. They prefer the tranquil beauty and inspiration of the older styles and are satisfied to stop their studies here and devote themselves to the creating of traditional arrangements. In the second phase of study you enter the field of modern arrangement and simple free-style which bring fresh flower designs other objects of interest which help bring about an interpretive quality. The third phase of the study of Japanese flower arrangement is advanced free-style which takes you into the realm of abstract design, *objet,* and *avant-garde.*

The terms modern, free-style, abstract, objet and avant-garde are confusing. Let me try to clarify. While free-style and abstract arrangements are classified as modern a modern arrangement need not be abstract. Likewise an abstract arrangement may be classified free-style but a free-style arrangement is not necessarily abstract. Similarly, although free-style is classed as modern, a modern arrangement need not be free-style. For instance many moribana arrangements are modern but are based on established patterns and are therefore not free-style.

It should be noted also that *rikka* and *shoka* may be interpreted in the modern manner. Complete freedom in the use of materials and containers is allowed but the basic design is retained.

We have discussed *rikka, shoka, nageire* and *moribana* in the preceeding pages. Now let us take a closer look at the different phases of modern arrangement.

81. *The modern container is a perfect foil for the rhythmic flowing lines of the plant material. The design is typical of the Adachi style of arranging flowers.*

Free-Style Arrangements *(jiyu-bana)*

A free-style arrangement is interpreted as any arrangement of good design created outside the basic patterns established by the various schools. The terms free-style, abstract, *objet* and *avant-garde* are often confusing and overlapping. In reality advanced free-style when interpreted as free expression encompasses them all. Unlike conventional forms, free-style is not limited to established designs and stated rules and offers the arranger infinite scope with materials and composition and permits the exercise of originality. It also allows one to interpret, design and create according to one's own vision and perception.

Free expression is the aim of both American and Japanese interpretation in free-style but to the trained eye there are many differences between a free-style arrangement by an Occidental with training in design principles and a student of *ikebana* with a background of years of practice in the basic patterns of his chosen school. *Ikebana* is more restrained in the use of material with fewer flowers and more thinning of foliage; it utilizes space to a greater extent; more attention is paid to the dimension of depth and there is more interest in shape and less in color; it shows a more sensitive feeling for material; accessories are seldom used in Japanese free-style.

Much thought is given to containers used in free-style arrangements. A vast supply of attractive, odd shaped, individually designed containers are created in Japan where the demand is great. They are made of pottery, bamboo, stone, metal, wood and other materials. Containers with multiple openings and paired containers (one tall and one low) are often used. Should the student be limited in his supply many beautiful arrangements can be made in containers from Western potters and in containers improvised from articles found about the home or in industry such as trays, bottles, baskets, cooking utensils and parts of machinery. Whatever the container used it should form an integral part of the design as a whole.

Often no container at all is used and the arrangement is placed directly on the floor or dais. Often coarse sand or crushed rock (sometimes sprayed a desirable color) is placed at the base and becomes part of the design. Bases such as bamboo, lacquer, or wood are seldom used in modern arrangement and then only if they enhance the arrangement.

In making abstract arrangements the designer may work with metal, wood, iron, concrete, feathers, plastics, glass, wire, or such bizarre materials as scrap metal, engine mufflers, wheels, cork, and other unexpected media. Floral materials are deftly worked into some of these abstractions as pure form and color without regard to their natural appearance.

The student who has studied conventional *ikebana* knows the value of following traditional patterns based on sound rules of design. His knowledge of line, form, texture, color harmony, and space will not only enable him to make many beautiful traditional arrangements but lead him into free-style based on his own creative ability. The principles absorbed from the old forms make the best possible foundation for the new.

After studying the simplicity of the arrangements of the traditional masters and the free and natural effects we are equipped to perfect our own free-style. The free-style approach (as the name implies) allows much room for self-expression. With free-style we can create an individual arrangement all our own unlike that of any other arranger. We are not limited by the type of container, choice of plant material nor past traditions. We are free to attempt unconventional compositions as long as our creation is beautiful, harmonious and founded on good design.

Although tradition still guides the eye and hand of the Japanese flower arranger and simplicity (even severity) is still the rule, the adherence to old patterns today is less rigid.

Abstract Arrangement *(chusho-bana)*

For the Occidental schooled in modern art, abstract flower arrangement seems neither strange nor incomprehensible. He recognizes that the motivating force is design which is the same in flower arrangement as in painting and sculpture and he sees the arrangement as an expression in pure form and design showing no resemblance to natural objects. Lines and shapes are the same in abstract as in other free-style but materials are more often non-floral. Abstract is free-style but free-style is not necessarily abstract. To clarify, an arrangement is free-style if it has similarity to nature but abstract if it is pure form and design. Abstraction is an art form which does not realistically represent nature. It begins with nature and abstracts certain forms and eliminates insignificant details. The flower arranger's purpose is to use form and design to dramatize an idea or mood.

There are many degrees of abstraction. Every flower arrangement is to a degree abstract. However, when we refer to an abstract flower arangement we

152

82. (Opposite, left) Japanese flower arrangements are not always linear—this one is a modern mass design. Note how carefully the materials are grouped.

83. (Opposite, right) Metal, bleached Scotch broom and tree fungus were used to create this abstract design.

84. (Left) An abstract design of rolled bleached wisteria and Scotch broom provides a delightful setting for two camellias in a black pottery container on a bridge base.

85. (Right) A brown pottery container, a root sprayed black, a black lacquer base edged in red and two red anthuriums were all that was needed for this dramatic arrangement. When the anthuriums faded they were replaced with one stalk of red gladiolus.

86. (Left) Black, red, and white dried materials are spiced by two yellow roses and clipped finger palm in a black pottery container.

87. (Right) An abstract design is displayed in a container designed by the Ohara School. The materials are calathea, three protea, and one ti leaf.

mean an arangement in which flowers (if used) are regarded as objects in the designed are and used for their color and shape without regard to their growth in nature.

The question often asked is "How can we learn abstract arranging?" The answer is simple. Develop the seeing eye and observe carefully, study conventional *ikebana* to gain a solid foundation for all arranging including abstract, and *practice*. One must have awareness of materials and understanding of all aspects of design: line, form, color, proportion, balance, depth, contrast, harmony, emotion.

154

Other developments in pure abstract forms are mobiles of paper, metal, bamboo, shells and wood which are interesting for their intricate design, motion, and balance; reliefs composed within frames and made of such elements as stones set in plaster, shells, seaweed, coiled wire, and dried flowers and plants; collages; and assemblages. These are designed often without the use of organic material and are sometimes used as backgrounds for true floral arrangements. The two though not actually related are viewed as one display.

Objet (From the French *objet d'art*)

This is a sculptured type of arrangement created in either wood, metal, or stone and used with or without flowers. Of all the types of Japanese arrangements this is perhaps the hardest for the Occidental, who has been accustomed to the use of many flowers, to understand. Many feel that this is another art form and is not flower arrangement. They fail to understand the motivating force inspired by the "awareness of nature," so much a part of the Japanese.

Mr. Sofu Teshigahara, headmaster of the large and modern Sogetsu School, is Japan's most avant-garde flower master and has been described as Japan's Picasso. This versatile artist has achieved world-wide acclaim for his exhibitions abroad, many of which have featured *objet*.

In commenting on this form of arrangement Mr. Teshigahara said, "Most people think of flowers and plants as being something delicate, fleeting, fragile, elegant, but in fact they are not so simple. At root they have an earthy animal quality that opposes, indeed threatens, mankind. It is my fascination with this demonic life-force that has led me to make these works." This shows the special view of the *objet natural* Mr. Teshigahara has discovered in plants and animal nature. Many of his arrangements of large gnarled roots are the embodiment of a brooding animal spirit. The catalysis of flower arrangement permits the artist to see both nature and *objet*.

Avant-garde (*zenei-bana*)

This term is generally used when referring to very new trends in the modern styles of arranging. *Avant-garde, objet* and most abstract arrangements are designed for exhibitional purposes only and are intended to be viewed as objects of art rather than decorative pieces. Perhaps there will come a time when these forms will be classified separately from pure flower arrangement.

In all creative expression there is a search for the new. *Ikebana* offers a most extensive media for this expression. *Ikebana* exhibits play an important role in providing examples and inspiration in this searching and discovery process.

There have been reports that the trend in *ikebana* is away from abstract and toward more naturalistic styles of flower arranging. Mr. Houn Ohara, head-

88. (Left) The large root which has a brooding animal spirit might be classed as an objet. It is in sharp contrast to the gentle spirit of the camellia flower and the ti leaves.

89. (Right) The sculptured feeling of driftwood has been heightened by a coating of gold paint. The modern black and beige container and black base contribute to the sculptured effect. Lilies and clipped palmetto bring a touch of naturalism.

master of the famous Ohara School, made this comment when asked whether there is a trend "back" to the naturalistic styles: "Yes, there is a trend toward the naturalistic, but it is not backward; rather, it is forward—a combining of naturalism with abstract. Great artistic expression can be given by adding the naturalistic to the abstract. While many persons think that the abstract is disappearing in favor of the naturalistic, I disagree. I feel that both are moving forward in combination with each other into a stage which is most appealing."

Whatever our individual reaction to abstract *ikebana* it is a vital force in flower arrangement. It is not displacing the traditional styles that have flourished for so long but it is making a place as a new branch of *ikebana*. If we are alert to changes of the times and willing to expand our perceptions it can bring excitement and fresh concepts of beauty to our flower arrangements.

Flower arrangement, like other living arts, is influenced by the age in which we live. The mood of contemporary life must be expressed—its emotions, progress, abundance and poverty. Today we live in an age of experimentation. Each new generation will add its own imprint to this art.

90. *(Left) This avant-garde arrangement is designed of furled aspidistra and tree branches. The container is an ancient bronze.*

91. *(Right) An ancient bronze container holds a traditional arrangement of azalea, hyacinths, and tulips.*

CONTAINERS

An old instruction book says, "A good hand or a bad hand at flower arrangement is evidenced by the combination of flowers and vase." A container may make or mar an arrangement. The combination of plant materials and container is a matter of design and since design is the most important factor in flower arrangement the selection of harmonious materials and containers is essential to a well-

92. *(Left) Pear branches and yellow tulips with red throats are used in a very old bronze container for a basic upright arrangement.*

93. *(Right) A contemporary* usubata *is used for a modern* shoka *arrangement of cattails and aspidistra.*

designed composition. The container is not just a vessel to hold water but an important part of the design as a whole.

In many modern arrangements no container is used at all. Dried material may be used either alone or with some non-floral objects such as glass slag, stones or wrought iron. Sometimes a small container or cup-holder is entirely concealed by flowers or plant material. In such an arrangement the container plays no part in the design.

94. *(Left) A lovely modern container holds camellia blooms while twisted roots curl around it. Crushed stone forms a base.*

95. *(Right) Stands and bases play an important role in classical arrangement. Note the interesting combination of container and base.*

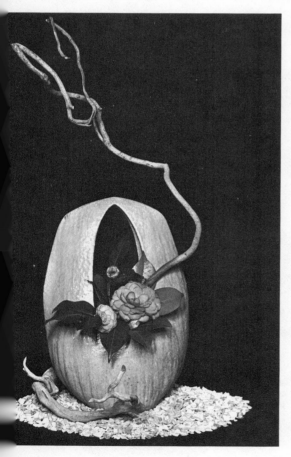

The numerous potters of Japan are producing excellent modern containers. In addition there are beautiful bronze and bamboo ones of more classical design. Exquisite old containers of Chinese and Korean origin can be found which may give inspiration to the arranger. However, numerous vases made by our own potters are of excellent design and are perfect for *ikebana*.

And don't be afraid to improvise. This has been done for centuries in Japan. The famous master of the tea ceremony, Sen-no Rikyu, once used a trout basket for flowers while on a fishing trip, and at another time he used a water bucket to arrange iris for a tea ceremony while on the battlefield!

96. (Left) A three-tierd bamboo container holds triple shoka *arrangements, all of different materials.*

97. (Right) Two well buckets were stacked to hold double shoka *arrangements of different materials. Well buckets and baskets have been used to hold flowers for centuries so why can't we improvise?*

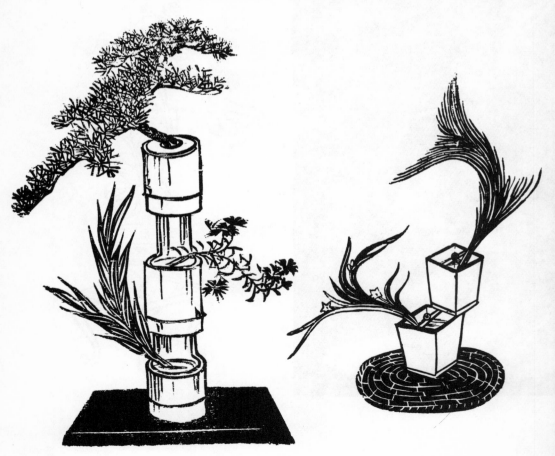

第四十　未生奥傳

舟の川法は凱舟釣舟等にて入舟は待人出舟は兄
送り登舟は上進にて降舟は下降の理なり凱舟は
陸にて通はず釣舟は水上にて通ふ如く流の枝
にて檣率ご見せ且は錨ご
見せて止り舟ご知るべし

第四十一
未生奥傳

月は滿つれば
かけるの習な
り依て三旬の
法を知るべし
上旬下旬は人の枝より
流しを用ひて左右に活
け中旬は留流しを後向
に用ゆべし水上はゑん
さんにて燒くべし

98. *Classical hanging arrangements have been popular in Japan since ancient times. Above are arrangements in two of the most popular containers, a
full moon and hanging bamboo boat. A half-moon container is often used too.*

IKEBANA FOR TABLE DECORATION

Few Japanese homes have a place for a table centerpiece. Several styles of *ikebana* may be adapted for table decoration although this use is more Occidental than Oriental.

When a table is placed against a wall and an all-around arrangement is not necessary, all forms of *ikebana* are beautiful and exciting. Many styles of *mori-bana* arrangements can be viewed from all sides and are charming on tables where a free-standing arrangement is needed. While Japanese arrangements are usually viewed from the front they must be correct when viewed from any angle. *Shoka* arrangements are tall, graceful, and can be seen through for easy conversation. By the addition of a flower or two or a bit of material to the back side they may be made free-standing and used as attractive table decorations. However, the material must not be added haphazardly but must be part of the design.

I have pointed out in the chapter on tray landscapes the use of *bonsai, bonseki* and *bonkei* as table decorations. Following are other Japanese floral forms particularly adaptable for table use.

Morimono

A *morimono* is an arrangement of fruit, fruit and flowers, fruit and vegetables, vegetables, or vegetables and flowers. It can be made in almost any kind of shallow or flat container such as a plate, tray, basket, mat or on a large natural leaf. *Morimono* literally means "things that are piled or heaped," but here we mean things that are arranged for decoration by the same principles and rules that are applied to flower arrangement. Arrange them artistically and utilize to advantage the beautiful colors and varied shapes to beautify the dining table. The most important thing in arranging a *morimono* is to decide which is to be the principal object among the materials used. When this is decided all other materials should be subordinated. Also, harmony in combining large and small or round and oblong shapes is important.

Fruit and vegetable arrangements are popular with the Japanese during harvest time and when flowers are scarce.

Floating Arrangement, *Uki-bana*

This form of arrangement is distinguished by plant material floating in water. Usually no *kenzan* is used; however, if it is necessary use a small one and then it is a simple matter to conceal it. There is beauty in the direct contact of the flower and water in floating arrangements. One not only sees the flowers but at the same time enjoys the surface of the water as well. The water adds a delightful sensation of coolness. This style harmonizes well with Western settings. Special care is required in harmonizing flowers and dish. Large flowers offer more interesting and striking variations than small ones. It is best to experiment with this type of arrangement without too much consideration of rules.

Spread Flowers, *Shiki-bana*

Another style of arrangement suitable for a centerpiece is the spreading arrangement, *shiki-bana*, in which flowers and leaves are arranged directly on a table without container, tray, needle-point holder, or water. These are especially charming for a luncheon or banquet when a large number of arrangements are used and uniform containers are not available.

Schools of Ikebana

At the present time there are hundreds of different schools of flower arrangement in Japan. The main principles are essentially the same in all schools as they all evolved from the Ikenobo School. The differences are slight and of little importance.

Following are a few pointers to help you select a school or schools to study.

The terms school and style should not be confused. *Ikenobo, Sogetsu, Ohara*, etc. are the names of different schools of flower arranging. *Rikka, shoka, (seika), nageire* and *moribana* are the styles of *ikebana*. Of the four styles *rikka* and *shoka* are classical and of the many schools in Japan today *Ikenobo* is the only one that teaches all four styles. *Shoka* (or *seika* as it is called in some schools) is taught by some other schools such as *Enshu, Koryu, Kodoryu, Misho*, etc. *Nageire* and *moribana* are taught by all schools and are the easiest to learn. The styles are similar in all schools. The chief differences are in the length and angles of the branches, the combinations of materials, and the names applied to lines.

Ikenobo, Sogetsu, and *Ohara* are the schools best known to Americans and each has branches in New York as well as all over Japan. However, there are other excellent and highly qualified schools. Following is a list of a few of these: *Adachi, Enshu, Ichiyo, Kodoryu, Koryu, Kyofu, Misho, Saga*, and *Shofu*.

All of the schools teach some of the traditional patterns of arrangement and the student is expected to master these and then go on and develop his own style.

In choosing schools to study it is a wise procedure for the student to observe the various schools and decide which appeals to him most. There is a leaning by many people toward the modern schools which teach only *nageire* and *moribana* forms, but the serious student of *ikebana* should include instruction in one school that teaches classical forms as well.

While it is stimulating and exciting to study *ikebana* in the land of its origin, it is not necessary to go to Japan to become a proficient arranger. There are many qualified teachers in this country, both Oriental and Occidental, with whom you can study. To gain information concerning teachers of Japanese flower arrangement in your area contact the Chapter of Ikebana International nearest you.

Ikebana International

In recent years interest in the Orient has gained momentum at an astounding rate. In the cultural exchanges between the East and West *ikebana* has been one of the arts most easily transplanted. It can be practiced anywhere in the world with whatever material that is at hand. It is this versatility that has made this Japanese art truly international. By the same token its universality created the need for its devotees to form some link with Japan as a continuing source of inspiration. It was this need that led to the founding of the organization Ikebana International in 1956 by Mrs. Ellen Gordon Allen. Its aims are "to stimulate, cultivate and perpetuate the study and practice of *ikebana* throughout the world."

Within the span of a few years Ikebana International has covered the globe. The United States has at the present time sixty-one chartered chapters with more being formed all the time. In areas where there is no chapter, individuals can become members at large of the Tokyo chapter and receive the valuable literature and information of the organization. For information concerning this you may write Ikebana International, C.P.O. Box 1262, Tokyo, Japan.

Throughout its long history *ikebana* has been enriched from generation to generation with new ideas and styles expanding its horizon and making it a vigorous and living art. It is unquestionably the greatest floral art the world has ever known.

Japanese Flower Arrangement and Flower Shows

In Japan flower shows are never competitive as ours are. The flower compositions are exhibited and admired for their beauty and interest and enjoyed as other forms of art. In the West flower shows are nearly always competitive; however, *The Handbook for Flower Shows* suggests that flower show schedules

99. (*Opposite*) *The container is called* shikainami (*gentle waves of the four seas*). *Papyrus, bamboo, and fairy roses are designed in the* shoka *manner.* (*Arranged by Mrs. W. B. Garrison.*)

should never include a class for Japanese flower arrangements or a scale of points for them unless the participating group includes members who have learned to understand the art through diligent study and there are judges available who have had adequate training in the specific school which is being interpreted.

Western flower shows do often include classes for "an arrangement in the Japanese manner," "an arrangement showing Japanese influence," etc. which frequently cause much dissatisfaction among exhibitors and concern among judges who are unable to cope with so many diverse styles, many of them quite apparently non-Japanese. The answer to this is to establish a noncompetitive *ikebana* section. The influence of and interest in Japanese flower arrangement is world-wide so a National Council standard show exhibiting classes of various types and styles of Japanese arrangements would be educational and these features would add variety and sparkle to a routine flower show. Think of all the possible classes the various styles and their several variations offer the exhibitor, and add to this the interpretation of the many schools of these styles! The schedule committee could spark jaded interest by bringing other qualities of things Japanese into the schedule. What could be more challenging than a class asking the arranger to express the highest sense of Japanese beauty, *shibui*, or the qualities of *wabi* and *sabi*? *Jimi*, *hade*, and *iki* also offer exciting possibilities for interpretive classes. The staging committee too could reap rich rewards and put zest into their settings by borrowing ideas from the Japanese. These are only a few possibilities. As you read this book I am sure you will come up with many exciting and original ideas of your own.

The arrangements in the following plates were made by the author: 54, 55, 61, 65-70, 77, 78, 82, 85-89, 91-94.

SO YOU ARE GOING
TO JAPAN
VI

You can go to Japan and live in Western-type hotels, eat Western-style food and live in an entirely Western manner, but by so doing you will see only the Westernized facade and disappointingly experience only "the new Japan." The average visitor spends one week in Japan and exposes himself primarily to the public face of impersonal Tokyo. He sees only the commercial, the crude and ugly. To know Japan and discover its depth you must invite the Japanese people to reveal its hidden beauty to you. Those who know the strength of Japanese traditions realize how thin-skinned the surface changes are. Most of the people especially in rural districts still live in furnitureless, unheated homes, sleep on straw-matted floors, and eat bowls of rice with chopsticks. Students of Japanese floral arts should approach Japan as a culture to be experienced and understood rather than a series of sights to be seen. He should become as deeply steeped in Japanese ways as a traveling foreigner can by eating, sleeping, and living Japanese thus taking a journey to a different viewpoint and gaining a better insight into the arts he has come to study.

JAPANESE ETIQUETTE

While it is quite unnecessary for a foreigner visiting Japan to try to copy the Japanese manner, an insight into the development of some of their unique customs will help bridge the chasm between East and West and promote better understanding. While the basis of true courtesy may be the same in every land, the superficial differences between Occidental and Oriental manners are so startlingly different that we may often fail to comprehend the good will meant by others and stand apart and be strangers only because of lack of understanding.

167

The exquisite manners of the cultured Japanese, particularly those of the women, betwitch and charm. In Japan there is no movement either of hand or foot that is not governed by etiquette. There is a form for sitting and for standing, for opening and closing a door (no girl will open a sliding door standing, she kneels), for presenting or receiving a gift, for bowing and for the position of hands in salutation. All these customs have a naturalness that training alone cannot produce. Inheritance undoubtedly contributes to the Japanese amiability of manner, daintiness of habit, delicate tact and the strange power to present outwardly only the best and brightest aspect of character. The wonder and beauty of old Japan is still evidenced in the present formality of manner which appears natural rather than acquired and instinctive rather than trained. The capacity to achieve such manners could only have been inherited from past experiences of centuries of people under stern discipline. The Japanese impart the strange and alluring charm of a vanished world and a society founded on ancestor worship. The ethics of their ancient Shinto religion demanded unqualified obedience to the customs of the family. Since ethics in family cult, community life, religion, and government were all the same, outside and inside his home the ancient Japanese actions were under suspicion and a single breach might cause him ruin. Extraordinary regulations and regimentation repressed all self-assertion and made self-sacrifice a universal obligation. During these early periods in Japanese history the whole life of an individual was ordered for him. His occupation, marriage, property rights, even what he wore and ate were settled by religious custom.

Everyone was rigidly trained from infancy in the etiquette of expression and deportment. Demeanor was most elaborately and mercilessly regulated, not merely as to obeisances (of which there were many grades varying according to class and sex), but even in regard to facial expression, manner of smiling, sitting, rising, standing, walking and even the way of breathing. At one period it was a mark of disrespect to betray by look or action any feeling of grief, anger or pain in the presence of a superior. It was not enough for the sufferer to deny his feelings—he had to convey the opposite by a pleasant smile and a quiet, happy tone of voice. They also had to be careful about the kind of smile; for instance, it was a mortal offence if the back teeth showed when addressing a superior. Women of the military class were required to show signs of joy when hearing that husband or son had died in battle.

Rudeness in the lower classes was punishable by death. The old Japanese term for a rude person was said to be "An other-than-expected person." Therefore, anyone going against the prescribed etiquette of the day was in danger of losing his life.

These and countless other restrictions once ruled this fairyland world and shaped the soul of it. The old kindliness and grace of manner that we see in cultured Japanese people charm us even though we know that these manners were cultivated, for thousands of years, under the edge of the sword. The smiles are no less winning because we have been told of ancient times when not to smile in the face of pain or tragedy would cost them life itself.

Of course Japan has its very seamy side also and its full share of vulgarians and insensitive people. I realize the danger of generalizing and attributing to a whole nation characteristics that we find in a cultured and educated few. Japan does present a double image and all conclusions are two-edged and subject to contradiction. However, the heart of Japan is still dominated by its classical past and it is by gaining an understanding and insight into the attitudes and sense of values that has produced the sensitivity and awareness of the Japanese that we can gain much to enrich our own lives. Here we may find clues that will help us recapture the tranquility, serenity, harmony, and peace of mind which the machine age has taken from us.

A visitor to Japan need not be overly concerned with Japanese etiquette. The Japanese are generally willing to make concessions to Western innocence and do not expect him to behave according to their code. However, it is courteous and to your advantage to observe a few basic principles of etiquette and to have some understanding of their behavior and why they behave as they do.

The chief thing to keep in mind at all times is the fact that most Japanese admire calmness and quietness to such a degree that even a reticent American may seem hectic to them. A flashy smile, athletic handshake, and stentorian voice (qualities that may be acceptable or even irresistible at home) are quite out of place in a refined Japanese setting. A visitor must make a conscious effort to slow down and practice restraint and self-induced serenity. Serenity is one of the greatest gifts Japan has to give our overexcited world.

The Honorable Bow

All salutations in Japan are expressed by bows. It is their way to greet each other, pay respect, express thanks, apologize, ask favors, and say good-by. Bows may be made standing or sitting. In either case they are one of three types. The deep bow, *saikeirei,* the highest form of salutation; the ordinary bow; and the light bow.

The Japanese dislike to be touched and to them a handshake is not agreeable. Therefore, greet them with a simple bow.

It's Better with Your Shoes Off

The first difference in customs one notes when visiting Japan occurs at the entrance to any purely Japanese establishment. This is the removal of one's shoes. The Japanese preoccupation with footgear and the constant switching of it is not just formality but a necessity and courtesy for the sake of cleanliness and care of the soft Japanese flooring and the *tatami* mats. The custom is not mystifying when one realizes that in this society one practically lives on the floor. In homes, inns, restaurants, museums, shrines, temples, and many shops you must observe the custom. Shoes that are easy to slip on and off (and sturdy enough for gravel paths) are desirable and will make the operations of taking off and putting on shoes easier.

A Japanese entryway is like a foyer designed as a sheltered shoe-changing area. It is lined with enough extra slippers for the use of all visitors. Sitting on the edge of the foyer one rests one's feet on a long flat stepping stone called *kutsunugiishi* (stone where shoes are taken off). This is quite tricky because the indoor slippers (these are soft-soled, heelless felt slippers) must never touch the stepping stone. Your shoes are left here until you leave the house. Inside the house the felt slippers must be removed before you enter any room covered with *tatami* mats. You walk on *tatami* only in stocking feet or *tabi* (washable fabric socks divided at the big toe like mittens). So that you don't scuff your stockings and to keep your feet warm in winter you might carry ankle socks to wear indoors.

Clogs are provided to enter the garden from the house. These have wooden soles that rock slightly and are very comfortable when walking across stones.

Graceful floor sitting is tricky for Western women. Tight skirts make it impossible. Full skirts are more comfortable and look graceful.

Table Manners

In eating a Japanese meal there are definite rules that the Japanese must follow. These need not alarm a visitor to Japan. Simply watch your Japanese friends and follow their lead. You will be so charmed by the beauty and enjoyment of the occasions that after only a few attempts with chopsticks you will even be able to manage eating your soup with them!

Before starting a meal a Japanese says the equivalent of "I shall begin eating" and makes a light bow. He then picks up his chopsticks and places them parallel to the edge of the table or tray with the tips lying on the chopstick rest.

Here Are Some Japanese Table Don'ts:

Don't pick up chopsticks until your senior or the guest of honor has taken his.

Don't take food from the soup without lifting the bowl from the tray.

Don't take up dishes on the right side with the left hand or those on the left with the right.

Don't pick up and bite off chunks of food that cannot be eaten in one mouthful. Pull them into smaller pieces with the chopsticks.

Don't use your own chopsticks when helping yourself from a serving dish. If there are no separate chopsticks for serving the food reverse your own and use the opposite ends.

Don't leave any rice uneaten in your bowl.

Don't fail to lay down your chopsticks and stop eating while being given a second helping. Chopsticks when not in use should always rest at the right side of the tray protruding beyond the edge of the tray about an inch.

When the meal is finished the chopsticks should be laid in the tray to indicate you are through. Then bow and say "thank you" to your host. Another point to remember as a guest at a dinner party is that the guest should sit as the host bids and when everyone is seated and the host's greetings are over, the main guest begins to eat. Only after the main guest has done so may the others take up their chopsticks.

Tips on Traveling in Japan

To savor things Japanese calls for a quite different travel approach from that used in visiting most other countries. A tourist in Europe can get some idea of the real life of a country by observing public places, home exteriors, and the people on the street. Japan does not live as outwardly as the West. Residential streets are quite unlike those in Europe or ours. They do not have sidewalks and front lawns and there is only a cursory pavement. They resemble our country lanes except they are bordered by solid fences of plaster, bamboo, or wood, ingeniously constructed in many patterns. These fences do not look forbidding, rather they make one curious. It is beyond these facades that the real Japan is revealed in delightful houses and gardens hidden from the street. That is where you want to get—behind the scenes. Seasoned travelers recognize the fact that the best procedure for getting behind the scenes in any foreign country, particularly in a closed society like Japan's, is to use your business or social contacts. If you have no personal contacts perhaps you have business or social associates with connections in Japan who will write letters of introductions and let your coming be known. Natives or friends on the scene can open magical doors to scenes and experiences you would not otherwise guess existed. When properly introduced the Japanese are embarrassingly hospitable and go to unbelievable lengths to see that you enjoy your visit in their country. It is customary to take a gift with you when you visit, but your host quite likely will give you a number of gifts.

The most important investment money can buy is the services of your own guide-interpreter. There is a language problem. English is not as well understood in Japan as you may have been led to believe. You will need a guide-interpreter with cultural awareness and a knowledge of gardens, flower arrangement, and everything that relates to your interests. One way to secure the services of such a person is through the Japan Travel Bureau. A guide is not only necessary for sightseeing and visiting gardens, but for acting as interpreter for flower arranging lessons and many other unthought-of services. He may even make the arrangements for your lessons. If he is knowledgeable and sensitive to your tastes he can unlock doors to all sorts of fascinating experiences. He will get you into the most interesting restaurants, order for you exquisite food, and help you shop. Numbered streets are rare in Japan and locations of addresses are loosely described. Even taxi drivers can't find their way around, therefore your guide will be needed to steer you.

THE JAPANESE INN, *YADOYA*

Do stay in Japanese inns, at least for a few nights, because they give you a chance to live as the Japanese do at home and they are about as far as an Occidental can hope to penetrate into Japanese life. They are usually small and have only five to twenty-five rooms. Many inns were once private houses of the nobility and the well-to-do and give you a chance to live with and observe the best in gardens and architecture. Japanese service is everywhere superb and is particularly outstanding in the inns.

True Japanese inns of distinction do not as a rule cater to foreigners. They are afraid of the gaucheries they will commit such as getting soapsuds in the bath water, dirtying and scuffing the *tatami* by wearing shoes in the house and placing toilet articles or suitcases in the *tokanoma*. Once you have lived in a Japanese inn you will understand the magnitude of these offenses. Money alone does not open the door either. To be admitted one needs the good services of influential friends.

Anyone attuned to American resort hotels, a shopping arcade, a red carpet, and a canopied doorman will be taken aback by the restraint of a Japanese inn. The whimsical Japanese habit of concealing prestige and wealth behind a humble front is typified in the restraint of an inn's decor. Except for the addition of room telephones, electric lights, electric fans in summer and electric heaters in winter traditional Japanese inns have not changed.

The Bath

Innkeepers are adamant about two procedures which you are definitely expected to observe because they exist for the purpose of cleanliness. They are the shoe removal custom and the Japanese way of taking a bath. Your innkeeper or your maid will give you proper instructions for taking a Japanese bath and despite what you may have heard to the contrary it is possible to have a Japanese bath in complete privacy. Some inns have rooms with their own private baths. In Japan soaping, scrubbing, and rinsing, all of which Westerners perform in the bathtub, must be conducted outside the tub. Bathroom floors are slatted and equipped with drains. You can stand or sit on a bench and use the *hinoki* (wooden bucket) to douse yourself. You must be thoroughly clean and rinsed before stepping into the bathtub. It is unpardonable to take soapsuds into the bath.

The tub itself is usually of wood and very deep and full to the brim with water much hotter than our usual bath water. There is a lid for the tub that you are expected to replace to keep the water from cooling when you have finished. Anyone used to tiled bathroom walls and plateglass showers will at first consider an all-wooden room with walls, ceiling, and floor of unpainted wood an unlikely place to take a bath. However, the velvety smoothness and fragrance of the cypress wood of the bathtub will delight you. The caress of the wood will forever more make the touch of an enameled tub frigid.

When you use a public bathroom remember that they are immaculately clean and a guest going to the convenience place is, according to etiquette, invisible!

There usually is no public lounge, lobby or restaurant in a Japanese inn. Meals are served privately in your room and there is no menu but you will be served an array of delectable native foods. The floor is covered with *tatami* so you never wear shoes. Doors have no locks so you will not need a key.

A good inn will begin giving you V.I.P. treatment the moment you arrive. Your maid will await you at the front door and will become your own private waitress, room-maid, laundress, and bellboy.

Your room will be of suite proportions and contain a vestibule, a living-bedroom and sometimes a dressing-room and private bath. The inner-room will include a *tokonoma* which contains a *kakemono* whose subject has been chosen for the season of the year or to hail your arrival. The *tokonoma* will also include a flower arrangement and perhaps some art object. Your maid will bring you tea, a clean cotton kimono (*yukata*) for lounging and for sleeping, and if the weather is cold, a heavy silk outer kimono called *tanzen* also.

The maid will prepare your bath and after the bath and dinner (which is served in your room) she will take from a closet layers of silk quilts which she places on the floor for your mattress (some inns provide a foam-rubber mattress and heating pads), then add more bright colored quilts.

When staying at a Japanese inn it is not customary for the guest to ask for rates when registering. It is considered ill-mannered to discuss money matters. The innkeeper considers he must offer his best hospitality regardless of how much he will be paid for it and that this is a personal favor and not a business deal. When you receive your bill it will not be itemized but you are supposed to pay it without discussion or dispute. Rates at a first class inn will run more than at a first class Western-type hotel, but chances are you will be delighted with the value you receive.

Tipping

Tipping is a delicate subject in Japan at all levels. In many hotels and restaurants a service charge is put on the bill. When tipping is done it should be presented concealed in an envelope and for finesse in tipping always use figures involving three, five and seven. Never use the inauspicious number of four. Generally taxi drivers are tipped only if you retain them for a half day or longer.

TOPSY-TURVYDOM

The wonder and delight I felt upon first experiencing the strangeness of things Japanese is difficult to describe. I was infused with a sensation of fantastic weirdness such as I have experienced before, in lesser degrees, when encountering the completely new and unfamiliar. Years of acquaintance through study of the fantastic world of the Japanese seems not to diminish the sense of strangeness or dull its alluring charm. Even the physical actions of the people are unfamiliar. Always the left is the right side, and the right side the wrong. The Japanese speak backwards, read backwards and write backwards. These differences startle, delight and baffle.

I have been told that no adult Occidental can really master the Japanese language, because to understand and be understood, it is not enough to learn thousands of Japanese characters, but one must think in directions totally foreign to our way. That is to say, one must think backward, upside down, from the inside out and altogether topsy-turvy.

Many Japanese customs are directly opposite to those of our world. In fact, if we assume they generally do things in reverse to our way, we will not be far wrong.

Japanese books end where Western ones begin, and footnotes are printed at the top of the page. The type generally runs from the top of the page to the bottom and is read from right to left.

The salutation and date come at the end of the letter. First the family name is written then the given name and finally the courtesy title.

When handing back change to a purchaser, the Japanese first hands over the biggest piece of money, in reverse to the American way of handing back first the coins, then the smaller bills and last the largest bills. In Japan the implication is that as long as you receive the major portion of change the rest is considered unimportant. Few Japanese ever count the small change when it is received. To do so is considered miserly.

In denoting directions the Japanese say east-north or west-south rather than north-east and south-west.

Japanese umbrellas are made of oiled paper on ribs of bamboo and carried handle down, by means of a ring or loop on top.

In making up accounts the figures are written first and the name of items next.

In the West, sets of things are usually counted by the dozen or half dozen. A Japanese set of cups, plates and the like are five or ten, never six or twelve.

When beckoning a person toward him, a Japanese puts out his hand, palm down and fingers waving toward the person he is beckoning.

When counting on his fingers he first stretches all his fingers out and then bends them down beginning with the thumb. When all the fingers are down at five, he turns up the little finger for six and goes on from there.

The Japanese man has precedence over the woman. He is served his meals first. In entering or leaving a room, a theater, car, elevator, etc., the man leads and the woman follows. The man seated on a tatami mat does not rise when a woman enters the room. However, as more and more people travel, and as Japan becomes more Westernized, there is a tendency for the younger Japanese men to observe the rule of ladies first. Since the end of the war some of the Japanese girls are demanding this.

Do not ask a negative question when talking to a Japanese. He will answer "yes" whether the question is affirmative or negative. If you ask, "Is it so?" he replies,"Yes, it is so." When asked "It is not so?" he invariably replies, "Yes, it is not so."

The Japanese girl slips the eye of the needle over the point of thread instead of putting the thread through the eye of the needle.

A carpenter pulls instead of pushes his extraordinary saw and plane.

Keys are turned to open or close a lock in what we consider the wrong direction.

In Japan the newcomer is the first to call on the neighbors. He also sends them a gift of *soba* (noodles).

It is very polite to show interest in the china being used—polite to the extent of turning it over to examine the back. I well remember my surprise when a Japanese visitor having dinner in our home turned over a plate and commented on the maker!

At a Japanese dinner party the host very often leaves before his guests. This practice results from the fact that Japanese dinners are seldom held at home. They are often stag affairs held in restaurants. Details are left up to the management of the establishment. The host merely indicates how much he is willing to pay. Most parties are given on expense accounts and some end up in much reveling with guests staying on to enjoy the company of the geishas. The host, not wanting to mar the happy mood of his guests, suddenly and quietly disappears.

A Japanese does not open a gift in the presence of the donor. He doesn't want to cause embarrassment in case the gift happens to be mediocre or not to his liking.

Few Japanese people have developed independent thought and action; they find it very difficult to make up their minds when the solution to a problem has not been predetermined by rule or precedent or by a superior.

The Japanese often make noises while eating and drinking, especially soup, and regard it as a mark of appreciation rather than bad manners.

The business men in the highly industrialized city of Osaka are so engrossed with business affairs, that instead of the traditional greetings when they meet they say, "Are you making money?"

When visiting a Japanese home or restaurant one is struck by the immaculate matted floors and the simple beauty and cleanliness of the interior, but when visiting a Western-style business office, one usually finds it untidy, the floor littered with cigarette butts, bottles, orange peels and other refuse. Most Japanese have not learned how to use Western-type rooms. Unless a floor is covered with straw matting (tatami) it is apt to be considered an extension of the sidewalk and littered accordingly.

A Japanese business man wears Western clothes during working hours, works in a Western-type office, but at home he removes his shoes, puts on a kimono, sits on the floor and sleeps on the floor.

A host often invites a caller to take a bath as soon as he arrives. This is looked on as gracious hospitality, comparable to an invitation to stay for dinner.

At a formal dinner party, speeches are made before dinner rather than after. The host makes a speech and the guest of honor responds. I have had the delightful experience of speaking on such occasions while seated on a cushion on the floor and speaking through an interpreter. However, I always wonder just what I said as it came out in translation.

The clothing of a Japanese woman folds left side over right, which is exactly opposite to that of an American woman. In Japan only the clothing of the dead is folded right side over left.

Instead of the number thirteen being considered unlucky in Japan the number four is looked upon with superstition. This is because the word four is associated with the word for death. Japanese hospitals have no room numbered four.

Japan is an alluring puzzle. It would be impossible to collect and fit all the parts of this bewilderment of complexities into one comprehensive picture. In this book I offer you my favorite things Japanese only as parts of the puzzle, the mystery and fascination that is Japan.

It has been said that when you find, after many years of study, that you cannot understand the Japanese at all, then you are beginning to know something about them.

GLOSSARY

The following guide to the pronunciation of vowels in Japanese words may be helpful: *a* as in China; *e* as in men; *i* as in machine; *o* as in obey; and *u* as in bull. A vowel is always articulated, even at the end of a word. The consonants are pronounced the same as in English.

Adachi.   A modern school of flower arrangement, founded in 1917.

Akino nanakusa.   The seven grasses of autumn.

Amado.   Rain doors.

Asagao.   Morning-glory.

Ashirai.   Derived from the verb *ashirau,* to decorate, adorn, or enhance. The term applies to any supporting branch in a flower arrangement.

Bonkei.   Tray landscape.

Bonsai.   Culture of miniature trees.

Bonseki.   Sand painting on a black lacquer tray.

Botan.   Peony.

Butsudan.   Buddhist family altar.

Byobu.   Characteristic Japanese folding screen.

Cha-niwa.   Tea garden.

Cha-no-yu.   Tea ceremony

Chigai-dana.   A part of the *tokonoma.*

Choca Adachi.   Headmaster of *Adachi-ryu,* a school of Japanese flower arrangement.

Chocho.   Butterfly.

Chusho-bana.   Abstract flower arrangement.

Daisen-in.   A Zen monastary with a famous garden.

178

Daitokuji. A famous Zen temple in Kyoto.

Do. Trunk or body. One of the nine principal *rikka* branches.

Do-bashi. Earth bridge.

Dozo. Fireproof storehouse.

Enshu-ryu. A classical school of flower arrangement.

Fukiagejima. Windswept isle in a Japanese garden.

Fukusa. Square piece of silk used for ceremonial occasions.

Fusuma. Doors in a Japanese house.

Futon. Pad used as a mattress when sleeping on the floor.

Ginkakuji. The Silver Pavilion.

Gogyo. The five basic elements, wood, fire, earth, metal, and water, which according to ancient times were the factors in the universe and in human life.

Gogyseki. The five natural shapes of stones.

Gyakugatte. Left-hand classical arrangement.

Gyo. Semi-formal style.

Hade. Bright colors, bold patterns, youthful exhuberance.

Hana. Flower and plant material.

Haori. Short overgarment.

Hasu. Lotus.

Hibachi. Charcoal burner.

Higatte. Left-hand classical arrangement.

Hikae. One of the nine principal branches of a *rikka* arrangement. Also a term used by the Sogetsu school for the tertiary branch.

Hinoki. Wooden bucket.

Hira-niwa. Flat garden.

Ho-o. Phoenix.

Ho-hokeyo. Secret Buddhist scriptures.

Hongatte. Right-hand classical arrangement.

Horaijima. Island of the blessed in a Japanese garden.

Hotei. Most popular of household gods.

Houn Ohara. Headmaster of the *Ohara-ryu.*

Ichiyo-ryu. A school of flower arrangement.

Ikebana. Flower arrangement.

Ikenobo. The oldest school of flower arrangement in Japan.

Iki. Stylish, clever and sophisticated.

In. Negative element of the two cosmic forces, *in* and *yo.*

Ishi-toro. Stone lantern.

Jimi. Sober, sedate.

Jiyu-bana. Free-style.

Kaiseki. Light meal served at a formal tea ceremony.

Kaishi. Paper squares used at a tea ceremony.

Kakeji. A calligraphy painting on a *kakemono.*

Kakemono.   Hanging scroll.

Kakezu.   A *kakemono* painting.

Kame.   Tortoise.

Kami.   Spirit.

Kamidana.   God-shelf in a Shinto shrine.

Karasu.   The black crow, symbol of filial devotion.

Kare-sansui.   Dry landscape.

Kenzan.   A needlepoint holder.

Kiakujinto.   Guests' isle in a Japanese garden.

Ki-dome.   The last grass or flower material added to an arrangement.

Kiku-no-go-mon.   Emblem of the Imperial family.

Kiku.   Chrysanthemum.

Kikyaku.   Earth. Reclining. One of the five shapes of stones.

Kinkakuji.   The Golden Pavilion.

Kirei.   Beautiful.

Kiri.   Paulownia tree.

Kirin.   Unicorn.

Koan.   Intellectual drill on an unsolvable question.

Kodo.   Incense ceremony.

Kodo-ryu.   A classical school of flower arrangement.

Koi.   Carp.

Koicha.   Thick pasty green tea used at tea ceremony.

Komi.   Crotch wedge for *shoka* arrangements.

Koryu.   A classical flower arrangement school.

Kotan.   Elegant simplicity.

Kubana.   Flowers for offering.

Kubari.   Stick for holding flowers in classical arrangements.

Kura.   Fireproof storehouse.

Kutsunugi-ishi.   Stone where shoes are removed.

Kyofu-ryu.   A school of flower arrangement.

Mae-oki.   One of the nine principal branches in a *rikka* arrangement.

Matsu.   Pine.

Mikoshi.   One of the nine principal *rikka* branches.

Mizugiwa.   Water's edge. Depth of water pertaining to a flower arrangement.

Misho-ryu.   A classical school of flower arrangement.

Momiji.   Maple.

Mono.   Peach.

Moribana.   Style of arranging flowers in a shallow container.

Morimona.   An arrangement of fruit and flowers.

Muga.   "It is not I that am doing this." A principle of the Zen religion.

Nagashi.   One of the nine principal *rikka* branches.

Nanakorobi-yaoki.   A phrase credited to Daruma which means "seven falls and eight rises."

Nageire.   Free and natural style of arranging flowers in a tall container.

Nejime.   A small cluster of flowers that form *tai*.

Noh.   Classical Japanese drama.

Ono-no Imoko.   Founder of the Ikenobo school of flower arrangement.

Oha.   Large leaves.

Ohara-ryu.   A modern school of flower arrangement.

Osaki-ni.   "Before you."

Oshi-dori.   Mandarin ducks.

Ozen.   Individual trays.

Reisho.   Metal. Low vertical. One of the five stone shapes.

Rikka or *Rikkwa.*   First formal style of flower arrangement.

Roji.   "Dewy path." Garden path. A part of a tea garden.

Rokkakudo.   Hexagonal Temple in Kyoto where flower arrangement as a formalized art was founded.

Roseitei.   Incense room.

Ryu.   School.

Ryu.   Dragon.

Ryoanji.   This Zen garden near Kyoto is perhaps the world's most famous garden.

Sabi.   Unobtrusive and patinated by age.

Saikeirei.   A deep bow.

Saga-ryu.   One of the very old schools of flower arrangement.

Sakaki.   Sacred tree of Buddhist religion.

Sake.   Japanese rice wine.

Sakkei.   Borrowed scenery.

Sakura.   Cherry blossom.

Satori.   Enlightenment.

Seika.   Classical style of flower arrangement.

Semba-suru.   Good luck symbol meaning one thousand cranes.

Sen-ei.   Present Headmaster of Ikenobo school who is forty-fifth generation in direct line from Sen-mu, founder of the school.

Sen-mu.   First Ikenobo Headmaster.

Sen-kei.   A fifteenth century Headmaster of Ikenobo school who did much to perfect *rikka* arrangement.

Sen-ko.   Thirty-second Headmaster of Ikenobo school.

Sen-O.   A sixteenth century Headmaster of Ikenobo school.

Sen-no Rikyu.   A famous tea master and master flower arranger.

Shibui.   Deepest and purest beauty word in the world.

Shibusa.   A noun with the same meaning as the adjective *shibui*.

Shichifukujin.   Seven gods of good luck.

Shigyo.   Fire. Arching. One of the five stone shapes.

Shika.   Deer, the messenger of Kasuga shrine.

Shiki-bana.   Style of arranging flowers by placing them directly on a table with no container.

Shin. The straight style, one of the three styles of classical arrangement.

Shin. Sincerity and truth. The principal branch in flower arrangement.

Shintai. Water. Flat or horizontal. One of the five shapes of stones.

Shinto. The native religion of Japan.

Shirasagi. The heron, symbol of purity.

Shobu. Iris.

Sho-chiku-bai. Pine-bamboo-plum, prominent luck symbol in all Japanese arts.

Shoin. Part of the *tokonoma.*

Shoji. Sliding doors of a Japanese house.

Shoka. Classical style of flower arrangement developed by the Ikenobo masters in the fifteenth century.

Shofu-ryu. One of the newer schools of flower arrangement.

Sho-shin. One of the nine principal branches of a *rikka* arrangement.

Shotoku Taishi. Regent to Empress Suiko and patron of Ono-no Imoko.

Shujinto. Master's isle in a Japanese garden.

So. Informal classical style of flower arrangement.

Soame. A famous sixteenth century tea master and designer of gardens.

Sode-gaki. A type of fence called sleeve fence.

Soe. The secondary line in a flower arrangement.

Sofu Teshigahara. Founder of Sogetsu-ryu.

Sogetsu-ryu. Large modern school of flower arrangement founded by Sofu Teshigahara.

Sukiya. Tea house.

Tabi. Japanese socks divided at the toe like mittens.

Tai. Tertiary branch of a flower arrangement.

Taido. Wood. Tall vertical. One of the five stone shapes.

Tai-shin. The *shin* of the *tai* group.

Takaramono. The most precious things.

Takemikazuchi. General in the legendary age of gods.

Tana. A part of the *tokonoma.*

Tango-no-sekku. Boy's festival.

Tanuki. Badger.

Tanzen. Outer kimono.

Tatami. Regulation floor mat in Japan.

Ten-chi-jin. "Heaven, earth, man." Terms sometimes used to denote the principal branches of a flower arrangement.

Tobi-ishi. Stepping stones.

Tokonoma. Ornamental alcove—a place of honor in a Japanese home where a hanging scroll, flower arrangement, and object of art are displayed.

Tora. Tiger, symbol of military prowess.

Torii. The gate before a Shinto shrine.

Toro. Japanese lantern.

Toyotomi Hideyoshi. One of Japan's outstanding generals of the sixteenth century. An enthusiastic tea votary and flower arranger.

Tsubaki. Camellia.

Tsuitate. A simple panel screen.

Tsukiyama-niwa. Hill garden.

Tsukubai. Purification basin in a tea garden.

Tsuru. Crane.

Tsurukame. Crane and tortoise combination which symbolizes good luck and longevity.

Uguisu. Bush warbler.

Uke. "To receive." One of the nine principal *rikka* branches.

Uki-bana. A floating arrangement.

Ume. Plum blossom.

Ushiro-gakoi. Branches which finish an arrangement in the back.

Usubana. A red lacquer stand.

Usubata. A flat-topped, wide-rimmed bronze flower container.

Usucha. Foamy tea served during the tea ceremony.

Wabi. Atmosphere of quietness and humbleness.

Wa-Kei-Sei-Jaku. Harmony, Respect, Purity, and Tranquility. The four qualities applied to the tea ceremony.

Yadoya. Japanese inn.

Yang. Positive element of the two cosmic forces.

Yin. Negative element of the two cosmic forces.

Yo. Positive element of the two cosmic forces, *In-Yo.*

Yoritsuki. Waiting room in the tea garden.

Yukata. Cotton kimono for sleeping and lounging.

Yukimi-doro. Small snow-viewing lantern.

Zen. Sect of Buddhism.

Zenei-bana. Avant-garde.

PHOTOGRAPHY CREDITS

All photographs by the author except as follows:

INDEX